Reflections on Creator God
50 Days of Devotion

**Missouri Association
for Creation**

Reflections on Creator God: 50 Days of Devotion
First printing: 2021

ISBN# 978-1-7923-5278-2

All Scripture references are from the New American Standard Bible unless otherwise identified.
NLT – New Living Translation
NIV – New International Version
NKJV – New King James Version

Please consider requesting that a copy of this volume be purchased by your local library system.

Devotionals were written by Marv Schaefer who has served as President of the Missouri Association for Creation since 2015.

The Missouri Association for Creation meets on the second Monday of every month at a location in the greater St. Louis area. Please visit mocreation.org for information.

Thank you to all of the wonderful Christian men and women who contributed to this devotional in so many ways.

Photo credits can be found at the end of this book.

Printed in the United States of America

To Jesus Christ.

"For it was the *Father's* good pleasure for all the fullness to dwell in Him, and through Him to reconcile all things to Himself, whether things on earth or things in heaven, having made peace through the blood of His cross." **Colossians 1:19-20**

Table of Contents:

Introduction

One of these four things is true:

1. Matter and energy do not exist.
2. Matter and energy are eternal.
3. Matter and energy sprang into existence from nothing.
4. Matter and energy were created.

These are our only options, there are no others.

Premise 1 is empirically false. We observe matter and energy every day.

Premise 2 and premise 3 are falsified by the laws of nature (as you will see as you go through this Devotional).

Premise 4 cannot be scientifically proven nor can it be disproven, making it the only one of the four premises that has not been falsified and thus, based on science, the only one that can be true.

The question, therefore, is not "Is there a Creator?" The question is "Who is the Creator?"

You certainly will not hear that from the science community. They are essentially holding on to premise 3 as the place from which the answer will <u>eventually</u> come. Please understand that this belief on their part is faith-based and is not supported by the known laws of nature. They don't believe it for scientific reasons, they believe it in spite of what empirical science clearly tells them... that there has to be a Creator.

Paul tells us in Romans 1:18-20 that God has made the truth evident to them and that they are without excuse:

18 For the wrath of God is revealed from heaven against all ungodliness and unrighteousness of men who suppress the truth in unrighteousness, 19 because that which is known about God is evident within them; for God made it evident to them. 20 For since the creation of the world His invisible attributes, His eternal power and divine nature, have been clearly seen, being understood through what has been made, so that they are without excuse.

Scripture tells us quite clearly that God exists in three distinct persons and that God the Father created everything through His Son, Jesus Christ, who is also upholding all of creation.

It is incredible, indeed, to consider the elegant symmetry and transcendent beauty of all that God created. It is beyond our ability to fathom the mind-boggling complexity of every living thing and the interrelationships necessary for it all to work together to sustain life. It is indeed miraculous.

The devotionals in this book are designed to bring glory to our Almighty Creator and to generate reflection on His creativity, His omniscience, His Divine power and His sovereignty over all things.

Our Creator is beyond compare. He is rightly due our praise and devotion.

Reflections on Creator God
50 Days of Devotion

**Missouri Association
for Creation**

Psalm 90:2:
Before the mountains were born or You gave birth to the
earth and the world, even from everlasting to everlasting,
You are God.

God exists outside of time. He is the Creator of time, which began with day one of the creation week. He chose Moses to write this Psalm and it was Moses who had recorded the creation account in the Book of Genesis.

Moses makes a very transparent statement here... God is eternal. He has never and will never not exist. Mountains are often used as a metaphor for age (Genesis 49:26, Deuteronomy 33:15, Habakkuk 3:6) and Moses tells us in this passage that God was here first and always.

> *Moses makes a very transparent statement here... God is eternal. He has never and will never not exist.*

The Law of Causality is a law of physics that has two premises:
1. Every effect has a preexistent cause.
2. The effect can never be greater than the cause.

Laws of nature are absolutes regarding the physical universe and in order to be considered a law there can be no known violations. Several obvious conclusions can be drawn here:

First of all, whatever caused the universe could not come from the universe itself because logically, the universe cannot preexist itself.

Secondly, the cause can't come from nature because whatever caused the universe would then also need a cause, and that would need a cause, etc. It would therefore be impossible to get back to a first cause.

It is indisputable that the first cause has to come from outside of nature and it unmistakably must preexist nature. Observable science dictates that the cause of the universe must come from outside the universe.

The first cause must be "from everlasting to everlasting". It can only be Almighty God.

Lord God, that You created it all is self-evident. True science can only confirm Your mastery. Glory and honor to You and only You. Amen.

Psalm 102:25-26:
"Of old You founded the earth, And the heavens are the work of Your hands. "Even they will perish, but You endure; And all of them will wear out like a garment; like clothing You will change them and they will be changed."

𝔗 he heavens and the earth will wear out "like a garment" but God will endure.[1]

It is interesting that the Psalmist used a garment as a simile for how the universe and everything in it will wear out. When the Israelites were in the wilderness, God miraculously preserved their clothing and their sandals (Deuteronomy 29:5). The natural tendency, though, as stated in this Psalm, is for everything to wear out.

Science calls this "entropy" and it is best explained by the Second Law of Thermodynamics. Dr. David Menton describes it this way:

The Second Law states that with time, everything in the universe tends to undergo progressive degradation. With the passing of time, things do not naturally increase in order and integrated complexity, they decrease.[2]

Essentially, energy is constantly being converted to an unusable state and at some point, the amount of usable energy in the universe will be exhausted. When that happens, the universe as it currently exists will suffer heat death.

Scripture and observable science tell us that the universe is headed down an unalterable path from order to disorder, yet the theory of evolution says that we are going from a chaotic event (the Big Bang) to the exquisite order that we see in all living things.

> *Scripture and observable science tell us that the universe is headed down an unalterable path from order to disorder.*

Actually, the hand of our Creator could not be more obvious and He is promising us a new heaven and a new earth to eventually replace the original.

German Physicist Rudolf Clausius formalized the laws of thermodynamics in the 19th century, some 2,800 years after the Creator of natural law had revealed it in scripture. He is an awesome God.

Lord God, we can trust Your word, it is truth from beginning to end. Thank You, Lord for so much revelation about what You have created, it is beyond our comprehension. Amen.

---

[1] Isaiah 51:6 also uses this terminology
[2] Essays on Origins: Creation vs. Evolution, David N. Menton, PhD, (Missouri Association for Creation 2016) p. 20

John 1:1-3:
In the beginning was the Word, and the Word was with God, and the Word was God. He was in the beginning with God. All things came into being through Him, and apart from Him nothing came into being that has come into being.

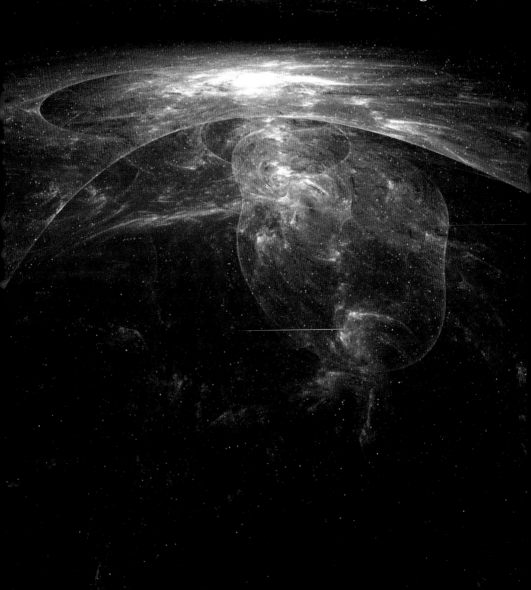

Scripture makes it very clear that God the Father created everything through His Son, Jesus Christ.

John repeats this important truth in verse 10:

"He was in the world, and the world was made through Him, and the world did not know Him."

The Apostle Paul expands on John's proclamation in Colossians 1:16 when he adds that Jesus created all things, "both in the heavens and on earth, whether visible or invisible". He further tells us in 1 Corinthians 8:6 that it is through Jesus that we live.

The writer of Hebrews declares in Hebrews 1:2 that not only did Jesus make everything, He is the heir of all things.

So, Jesus Christ, at the direction of the Father, created the universe and everything in it, displaying its magnificent splendor for all to see. Then, in total submission to the Father, He was inserted into history, took on human flesh and died a horrific death in order to save that which He had Himself created in His own image.

> *The one who created us, died to redeem us. This is love of the highest order... both for His Father and for us.*

The One who created us, died to redeem us. This is love of the highest order... both for His Father and for us.

Romans 10:9 says:
that if you confess with your mouth Jesus as Lord, and believe in your heart that God raised Him from the dead, you will be saved;

Redemption is available only through Him. The gates of heaven were opened to us through His incredible sacrifice. Our only responsibility is to accept this remarkable gift that He has given us.

Jesus, You are worthy of the highest praise and honor. We are ever mindful of the totality of who You are: Awesome Creator, Crucified Saviour and Risen King. We look ever forward to Your return and to eternity in Your presence. Amen.

Psalm 33:6:
By the word of the LORD the heavens were made,
and by the breath of His mouth all their host.

The words "God said" appear eight times in the creation account in Genesis 1.

This Psalm reiterates that God's spoken word is responsible for all of creation and that it was brought into being from absolutely nothing!

Imagine having the power to speak something into existence. Now imagine having the power to speak this universe into existence and having the wisdom and creativity to make it all work together and to give us everything we need for life.

The Word of God is powerful... and God has given us His word in scripture as a guidepost for our life.

2Timothy 3:16 (NIV) says:

All Scripture is God-breathed and is useful for teaching, rebuking, correcting and training in righteousness.

Just as the power of God's word spoke everything into existence, His word has the power to transform our lives.

It is no coincidence that the Apostle John refers to Jesus as "The Word". Scripture tells us with absolute clarity that God created all things through His Son, Jesus Christ (John 1:3,10, 1 Corinthians 8:6, Colossians 1:16, Hebrews 1:2) so when John refers to Jesus in this manner, he is affirming Him as Creator.

> *Just as the power of God's word spoke everything into existence, His word has the power to transform our lives.*

The gospels give us many examples of the power of Jesus' word:

The power of His word healed the Centurion's servant (Matthew 8:13). The power of His word brought Lazarus back to life (John 11:43) and the power of His word brought salvation to the thief on the cross (Luke 23:43). Even the wind and the waves obey Him.

Deuteronomy 8:3 tells us that *"man shall not live by bread alone, but on every word that proceeds out of the mouth of God."* Jesus quoted this verse to Satan when He was being tempted in Matthew 4.

Bread satisfies a temporal need. God's word not only ministers to our spiritual needs, its rewards are eternal.

Lord God, we thank You that we have Your Word in written form and that we may read it, study it and understand it. Every encounter we have with scripture brings us closer to You. Amen.

Genesis 1:1:
In the beginning God created
the heavens and the earth.

$\mathcal{T}$he very first passage in scripture makes a very simple, yet very profound statement. God is responsible for creation.

"Created" in this passage is the Hebrew word *bara*, which means "created out of nothing", so creation involved the act of instantaneously bringing into being matter which did not previously exist.

When an artist struggles to capture a magnificent seascape or a majestic snow-capped mountain, he is merely attempting to replicate the awe-inspiring beauty of something that Almighty God created from a blank slate.

Simply put, when God started the process of creation, there was nothing. Nothing to model. Nothing to replicate. Nothing from which to draw ideas... there was nothing. The beautiful tapestry and the astonishing complexity that He wove together is beyond human comprehension and it serves to glorify the One who created it.

> *When an artist struggles to capture a magnificent seascape or a majestic snow-capped mountain, he is merely attempting to replicate the awe-inspiring beauty of something that Almighty God created from a blank slate.*

The Hebrew word for God in this passage is *Elohim*. The Discovery Bible Lexicon says this:

(*Elōhîm*) expresses *Yahweh* (The Eternal God) is in charge of *every* circumstance as *the* Creator, *the* all-powerful One establishing all the physical scenes of life. This divine title is an emphatic plural in Hebrew to dramatically convey *Yahweh* as *always in charge – whose plan always triumphs!*[3]

He created all things and He is in control of all things. He is most worthy of praise and exaltation.

Lord God, when we consider the splendor of a sunset, or the calm serenity of a country lake, we know that these things only reflect the magnificence of the One who created them. Amen.

---

[3] HELPS Ministries, Inc, *The Discovery Bible, HELPS Lexicon.*

Colossians 1:16:
For by Him all things
were created, both in the
heavens and on earth,
visible and invisible,
whether thrones or
dominions or rulers or
authorities—all things
have been created through
Him and for Him.

*E*ven the invisible things were created through Jesus and for Jesus. During His time on earth, the only way to communicate with people who were separated by great distances was to dispatch a messenger. It took long periods of time to complete the connection.

Today, we can communicate in real time with someone on the other side of the world.

The telegraph was invented by Samuel Morse in 1844. While this didn't provide an instantaneous connection, it reduced the time to a few hours. The telephone was a vast improvement, invented by Alexander Graham Bell in 1876.

Today, we can have virtual meetings via the internet with people all over the world participating and using charts, slides and videos to illustrate important points.

> *It is truly astonishing to consider that everything necessary for this type of communication was an invisible part of the original creation.*

It is truly astonishing to consider that everything necessary for this type of communication was an invisible part of the original creation. God gave us every tool from the very beginning. What remained was for man to discover and utilize them.

In Revelation 11:9, God tells us of the two witnesses who will lie in the street for 3 ½ days and that *"all peoples, tribes, languages, and nations will stare at their bodies."* (NLT).

This was inconceivable when John penned the Book of Revelation (approx. 96 AD) but it didn't need to be possible then.

Today, man has discovered what God had ordained in the very beginning. It is not only possible for the world to see the witnesses, it is inevitable. God had provided the means to do so from the very beginning.

Lord God, we are more amazed by You every day. There is nothing that You have not ordained, there is nothing that You have told us that will not come to pass. Give us the heart to serve You all the days of our lives. Amen.

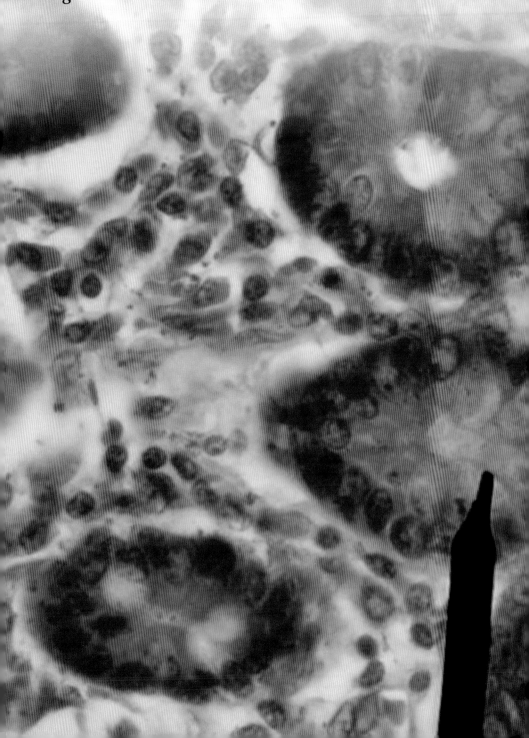

Hebrews 11:3:
By faith we understand that the worlds were prepared by the word of God, so that what is seen was not made out of things which are visible.

The power of His word is on display in everything He made and His creativity and wisdom, especially in the creation of life, are astonishing.

The cell is something that is not visible to us except through a high-powered microscope. It is a wondrous thing to behold.

Walter Bradley is a PhD material scientist who was interviewed by Lee Strobel for his book *The Case for Faith*. He described a single-cell organism as more complicated than anything that can be recreated through the use of supercomputers. He then characterizes that one-cell organism as a high-tech factory that features:

Artificial Languages	Information Retrieval Systems
Decoding Systems	Proof-reading Mechanism
Memory Banks	Quality Control Mechanism
Assembly Systems	Prefabrication/Modular Construction
Control Systems	High-Speed Replication System

Just one of these features by itself shouts design. Taken in its totality, it is screaming "Master Design".

Those who believe that there is no Creator and that the first living, functioning cell sprang into existence in a "primordial soup" millions of years ago with no intelligent cause are making an inherently unreasonable assertion.

> *He described a single-cell organism as more complicated than anything that can be recreated through the use of supercomputers.*

Remember that Bradley's description is of a one-cell organism. The number of cells in the human body is estimated to be over 37 trillion, a number far beyond our comprehension.

Our all-powerful and omniscient Creator is beyond compare and most worthy of unending praise.

Lord God, Your works are masterful and truly beyond our understanding. Life is truly miraculous and could only have been ordained by You. Amen.

Jeremiah 33:25:
But this is what the LORD says: I would no more reject my
people than I would change my laws that govern night and
day, earth and sky. (NLT)

*A*lthough today's verse is principally about God's fidelity to Israel, He also clearly tells us that He has ordained the physical universe and the laws that govern it as well. These laws of nature, absent God's intervention, are immutable, reflecting the very character of God and pointing quite dramatically to their majestic Creator.

Laws of nature have been in place since the instant that God spoke it all into existence. They beautifully point the way to the One responsible for the symbiotic beauty of it all.

Consider this… the laws of thermodynamics and the law of the conservation of matter inform us that by natural processes, matter and energy can neither be created or destroyed. Nature, therefore, cannot be responsible for the existence of either. They must exist at the direction of a powerful force that exists outside of nature.

> *When we consider the awesome power and wisdom of the Creator, we are awestruck that He is using these laws to sustain it all.*

When we consider the awesome power and wisdom of the Creator, we are awestruck that He is using these laws to sustain it all (Colossians 1:17, Hebrews 1:3).

The laws of gravity and motion are examples. They allow us not only to predict the paths of the moon and planets but to place satellites in orbit. Those very satellites have given us a glimpse of the incomprehensible magnitude and precision of the universe. God has allowed us to discover natural laws to help us understand not only the immensity of what He has done but also the brilliance required to ordain and maintain the intricacies and complexities of all that He created.

Albert Einstein's reflection is right on point: *"The Harmony of Natural Law reveals an intelligence of such superiority that, compared with it, all the systematic thinking and acting of human beings is an utterly insignificant reflection."*[4]

Lord God, Your power and glory are beyond our understanding. All of creation bows before You in awe. Thank You for revealing Yourself to us through what You have created. We are humbled before You. Amen.

---

[4] Albert Einstein (2011). "The World As I See It", p.28, Open Road Media

Genesis 1:2:
The earth was without form, and void; and darkness was on the face of the deep. And the Spirit of God was hovering over the face of the waters. (NKJV)

$\mathcal{T}$he very first day, God created water. In fact, the earth was covered completely with it, land did not appear until day three (Genesis 1:9).

There was water before there was light, before the sun, moon & stars and before plants, animals and humans. God, in his infinite wisdom created water first... life itself is not possible without it.

- 65% of our bodies are made up of water.
- The human brain is 70-75% water, and lack of water affects our cognitive process.
- Water transports nutrients through our bodies to our muscles and tissues.
- Water flushes our bodies of waste products.
- Water protects our vital organs, including our brains and our spinal cords.
- Water regulates our body temperature.
- Without water, a human could not survive for more than a few days.

> *God, in his infinite wisdom created water first... life itself is not possible without it.*

Water is needed to grow the plants that we eat & clean the clothes that we wear (and ourselves). It is often used to cook the food that we eat and of course, we love to swim in it.

How much water is there here on earth? Dr. Jonathan Sarfati tells us:

If the world's land masses were flattened and the ocean basins lifted to even out the earth's crust, the amount of water currently on earth would cover the entire globe to a depth of about 2.7 kilometres (1.67 miles).[5]

Philippians 4:19 tells us that our God will supply all of our needs. Our most important physical need is water. He made that first.

Thank you, Lord God for Your incomparable wisdom. You knew before anything existed what was needed first and foremost to sustain life and it was the first thing that You spoke into existence. You are indeed an awesome God! Amen.

[5] https://creation.com/the-wonders-of-water

Psalm 135:7:
He causes the vapors to ascend from the ends of the earth;
Who makes lightnings for the rain,
Who brings forth the wind from His treasuries.

hat Scripture describes in this passage is referred to by scientists as the hydrologic cycle.[6]

This really is a marvel of God's creative genius. Wikipedia describes it this way:

The central theme of hydrology is that water moves throughout the Earth through different pathways and at different rates. The most vivid image of this is in the evaporation of water from the ocean, which forms clouds. These clouds drift over the land and produce rain. The rainwater flows into lakes, rivers, or aquifers. The water in lakes, rivers, and aquifers then either evaporates back to the atmosphere or eventually flows back to the ocean, completing a cycle [7]

During this cycle, water can be found in three different states: liquid, solid or gas. Although they can be transformed from one state to another, water molecules never cease to exist.

That means that the water that God brought forth from the rock at Meribah, the water that John the Baptist used to baptize Jesus and the water that Jesus turned into wine are all still here today. What an absolutely amazing truth!

> *That means that the water that God brought forth from the rock at Meribah, the water that John the Baptist used to baptize Jesus and the water that Jesus turned into wine are still here today.*

Here's another truth: The first description of the hydrologic cycle in scripture was in the Book of Job:

For He draws up drops of water, which distill as rain from the mist, Which the clouds drop down and pour abundantly on man. (Job 36:27-28)

French engineer Bernard Palissy is given credit for discovering the hydrologic cycle in the 16th century, over 2,500 years after God first told us about it in scripture. Our Creator is wondrous.

Lord, it is astonishing to consider Your genius in creation and the intricate way that it all works together to sustain life. The more we learn, the more we are in awe. Amen.

---

[6] See also Amos 9:6 and Job 36:27-28.
[7] https://en.wikipedia.org/wiki/Hydrology

Bradford County
Courthouse Annex

1: THOU SHALT HAVE NO OTHER GODS BEFORE ME.

2: THOU SHALT NOT MAKE UNTO THEE ANY GRAVEN IMAGE.

3: THOU SHALT NOT TAKE THE NAME OF THE LORD THY GOD IN VAIN.

4: REMEMBER THE SABBATH DAY, TO KEEP IT HOLY.

5: HONOR THY FATHER AND THY MOTHER.

6: THOU SHALT NOT KILL.

7: THOU SHALT NOT COMMIT ADULTERY.

8: THOU SHALT NOT STEAL.

9: THOU SHALT NOT BEAR FALSE WITNESS.

10: THOU SHALT NOT COVET.

THE TEN COMMANDMENTS

...the government of the United States of America is not in any sense founded on the Christian Religion...

Article 11, Treaty of Tripoli.
The treaty was sent to the U.S. Senate,
where it was read aloud in its entirety and
approved unanimously. President John
Adams signed it and proclaimed it to the
nation on June 10, 1797.

An atheist believes that hospital should be built instead of a church. An atheist believes that a deed must be done inste of a prayer said. An ath strives for involvement in life and not escape into death. He wants diseas conquered, poverty banished, war eliminate

Madlyn Murra

American Atheists

Psalm 14:1:
The fool has said in his heart, "There is no God." They are
corrupt, they have committed abominable deeds; There is no
one who does good.

*H*ow do some people look at the world around them, indeed the universe surrounding them and come to the conclusion that it is all happenstance with no rhyme or reason? That it all kind of came together over billions of years with no plan, no direction and definitely no purpose.

Stephen Hawking, who passed away in 2018, was a world-renowned theoretical physicist and cosmologist who was celebrated by his peers. A USA Today column in 2011 quoted Hawking:

"The universe likely 'popped into existence' without violating the known laws of Nature,"[8]

This view is his explanation of how the universe came to exist without a Creator. Please understand that it is not based on empirical evidence. It is, in fact, spiritual in nature reflecting our ongoing battle in this world. (2 Corinthians 4:4).

What he believed was in spite of what he observed, not because of it. "Popping into existence" as Hawking put it, would be a glaring violation of natural law.

Evolutionary biologist and atheist Richard Dawkins agrees with Hawking:

"The universe that we observe has precisely the properties we should expect if there is, at bottom, no design, no purpose, no evil, no good, nothing but pitiless indifference."[9]

In the life of an atheist, this worldview is a sad reality.

Life's three great philosophical questions are: "Where did I come from, why am I here and where am I going?"

To an atheist, the answers are distressing: "I came from nothing, I'm here for no reason and I'm going nowhere."

To a Christian, the answers are full of hope and expectation: "I am created in God's image, I am here to glorify and honor the One who created me and my destination is heaven."

Thank You, Lord God that You have chosen us out of this world and given our lives meaning and purpose. Give us strength to live for Your glory every day of our lives. Amen.

---

[8] http://www.usatoday.com/tech/science/columnist/vergano/2011-07-31-stephen-hawking-creation-curiosity_n.htm
[9] Richard Dawkins, *River Out of Eden: A Darwinian View of Life* (Basic Books: 1995) p. 133

Psalm 104:24:
O LORD, how many are Your works! In wisdom You have made them all; The earth is full of Your possessions.

he totality of what God created is overwhelming to the author of this Psalm. He just can't contain himself and makes a proclamation: The works of God are countless, He wisely made everything and it all belongs to Him.

Proverbs 3:19 says:

The LORD by wisdom founded the earth, by understanding
He established the heavens.

God's wisdom is on display in the masterful things that He created on this earth and in the heavens above. In all of it, our lives are the most precious to Him. It is an incredible truth that for complex life to exist at all, every one of these must be present:

A G2 Star (the sun)	Wind
Location in a habitable zone	Tectonic Plates
Magnetic Field	Plants
Seasons of the Year (the moon)	Chemical Elements
Gravity	Atmosphere/Ozone
Soil	Liquid Water

A planet missing even one of these things cannot sustain life. A planet that has all these things cannot initiate life. Only God can do that.

Paul sums it up for us:

For by Him all things were
created, both in the heavens and on earth,
visible and invisible, whether thrones or
dominions or rulers or authorities—all
things have been created through Him
and for Him. He is before all things, and
in Him all things hold together.
(Colossians 1:16-17)

> God's wisdom is on display in the masterful things that He created on this earth and in the heavens above. In all of it, our lives are the most precious to Him.

God created it all through Jesus and for Jesus, it is all His possession and it is He that sustains it. Just as the Psalmist is overwhelmed, so also are we.

Lord God, how prodigiously wise You are and how stunningly exquisite is Your creation. We bow down in gratitude! Amen.

Genesis 1:3-5:
Then God said, "Let there be light"; and there was light. God saw that the light was good; and God separated the light from the darkness. God called the light day, and the darkness He called night. And there was evening and there was morning, one day.

On the very first day, God created light. But what was the light? He didn't create the sun and moon until the fourth day. The light that He established on day one was sufficient to light the earth because the verse tells us that He separated the light from the darkness and it also tells us that *"there was evening and there was morning"*. One day would require a light source and one rotation of the earth.

In order to create light on that first day, God also had to create the conditions for light to exist.

First consider that God created four things on the first day: time, space, matter & light.

Light is both a particle (matter) and it is part of an electromagnetic wave (energy). The light source produces many different wavelengths of energy (the light spectrum) and only a small part of that spectrum is visible to the human eye.

> *In order to create light on that first day, God also had to create the conditions for light to exist.*

Light has been a perplexing thing in the field of physics. In the 17th century some of the most prominent physicists believed that light did not travel at all and that it was instantaneous. Since then numerous scientists have measured the speed of light. The current consensus is that it travels at 186,000 miles per second, although that consensus is being challenged today by a few scientists who believe that the speed of light has been slowing down since the beginning of the universe.

So complicated to understand, yet created by the uncomplicated breath of God! So, what was the light on day one? The Book of Revelation gives us a hint by telling us what that light will be in the New Heaven and the New Earth:

And there will no longer be any night; and they will not have need of the light of a lamp nor the light of the sun, because the Lord God will illumine them; and they will reign forever and ever.
(Revelation 22:5)

Lord God, You are the Light. Your Son is described in scripture as the Light of the World. Your wisdom and power are beyond our grasp. We anxiously await the New Heaven and Earth! Amen.

Genesis 1:9:
Then God said, "Let the waters below the heavens be gathered into one place, and let the dry land appear"; and it was so.

$\mathcal{T}$his occurred at the beginning of the third day and must have been a cataclysmic event that reshaped the earth's surface. It would have formed basins for the oceans and high areas that would have been revealed (*let the dry land appear*) when the waters retreated to those basins, forming oceans, lakes and rivers.

Psalm 104 is an ode to God's power in creation. The Psalmist describes these events in verses five through nine:

5He established the earth upon its foundations, so that it will not totter forever and ever.
6 You covered it with the deep as with a garment; the waters were standing above the mountains.
7 At Your rebuke they fled, at the sound of Your thunder they hurried away.
8 The mountains rose; the valleys sank down to the place which You established for them.
9 You set a boundary that they may not pass over, so that they will not return to cover the earth.

> *Most importantly, it provided a place for God's primary creation, man, to dwell, to grow food and to go forth and multiply, filling the earth.*

The land that appeared had the rich soil and all of the nutrients necessary to sustain the plants that would be created later that same day. The soil would also process and recycle those nutrients so that living things would be able to use them continuously.

The trees would provide a habitat for the birds that would be created two days later on day five and along with other plants would provide 50% of the oxygen necessary to sustain life.

The land would provide a habitat for the beasts of the earth that would be created on day six. First and foremost, it provided a place for God's primary creation, man, to dwell, to grow food and to go forth and multiply, filling the earth.

Everything in God's creation is dependent on something else in God's creation. Most importantly, we are dependent on Him.

Lord, You prepared it all in a sustainable fashion to support the life of all that You created. Give us the wisdom to properly preserve it all until You take us home. Amen.

Psalm 8:6-8:
You make him to rule over the works of Your hands; You have put all things under his feet, all sheep and oxen, and also the beasts of the field, the birds of the heavens and the fish of the sea, whatever passes through the paths of the seas.

MATTHEW FONTAINE MAURY
PATHFINDER OF THE SEAS
THE GENIUS WHO FIRST SNATCHED
FROM OCEAN AND ATMOSPHERE
THE SECRET OF THEIR LAWS.

BORN JANUARY 14TH, 1806
DIED AT LEXINGTON, VA., FEBRUARY 1st, 1873
CARRIED THROUGH GOSHEN PASS TO HIS FINAL
RESTING PLACE IN RICHMOND, VIRGINIA.

EVERY MARINER
FOR COUNTLESS AGES,
AS HE TAKES HIS CHART TO SHAPE
HIS COURSE ACROSS THE SEAS,
WILL THINK OF THEE

HIS INSPIRATION HOLY WRIT
PSALMS 8 & 107. VERSES 8. 23 & 24.
ECCLESIASTES CHAP. 1. VERSE 8.

A TRIBUTE BY HIS NATIVE STATE
VIRGINIA.
1923

avid wrote this hymn of praise to the Creator, which focuses on the role that man plays as God's representative here on earth.

Verse 8 of this Psalm contains the phrase *"Whatever passes through the paths of the sea."* There is a wonderful story of scientific discovery that is attached to that part of the passage.

Matthew Maury was a retired Naval Officer and a Christian who lived in the 19th century. Maury had an intense desire to study and understand the Word of God and when he read this passage, he understood it to mean that the oceans must have currents that create pathways for ocean vessels.

He was determined to find them and diligently studied not just the oceans but also navigation, meteorology and wind currents. He did indeed discover pathways in the seas and he painstakingly charted and catalogued them so that sailors could take advantage of what he had discovered.

> *He did indeed discover pathways in the seas and he painstakingly charted and catalogued them so that sailors could take advantage of what he had discovered.*

This is from the website of the National Museum of the U.S. Navy:

Nicknamed "Pathfinder of the Seas," Matthew Fontaine Maury made important contributions to charting wind and ocean currents. His studies proved that by following the winds and currents ships could cross the ocean in fewer days than ever before.[10]

His studies also proved that following the Word of God can lead to great discoveries.

Lord God, thank You for God-fearing men like Matthew Maury who are tireless in their pursuit of truth and who serve as an example for us long after they have left us for eternity in the Kingdom. Amen.

---

[10] https://www.history.navy.mil/content/history/museums/nmusn/education/distance-learning/to-the-ends-of-the-earth/navigation/biography--matthew-fontaine-maury.html

Isaiah 45:18:
For this is what the Lord says, He who created the heavens
(He is the God who formed the earth and made it, He established it and did not create it as a waste place, but formed it
to be inhabited):

"I am the Lord, and there is no one else."

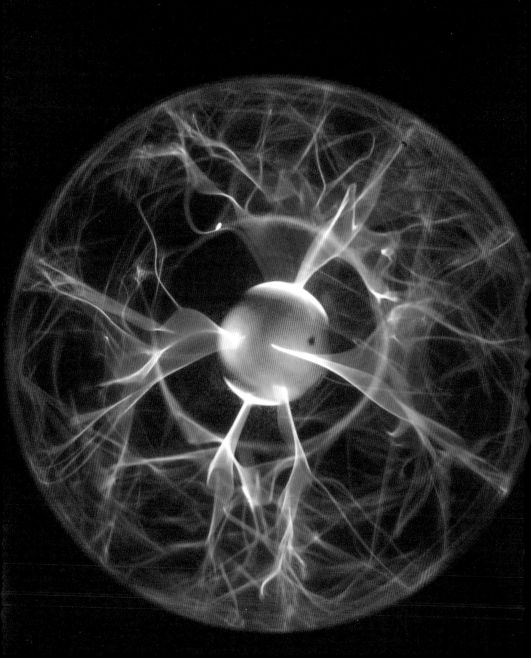

$\mathcal{I}$n his book, *God: The Evidence,* Patrick Glynn defines the anthropic principle this way:

"All the seemingly arbitrary and unrelated constants in physics have one strange thing in common – these are precisely the values you need if you want to have a universe capable of producing life"[11]

Today's scripture passage sums it up rather nicely. God specifically formed the earth to be inhabited. Therefore, all of those physical constants to which Glynn referred in the above quote did not come about randomly over billions of years as the secular worldview dictates. The probability of that is so mind-bogglingly infinitesimal that it is an absurdity.

Fine-tuning demands a fine-tuner. This passage identifies Him unequivocally... And God fine-tuned it specifically for us, then charged us with its care.

These physical constants include things like:

Gravitational Force	Proton Mass
Electromagnetic Force	Electron Mass
Strong Nuclear Force	Cosmological Constant
Weak Nuclear Force	Mass Density of the Universe

According to Dr. Robin Collins, who was interviewed by Lee Strobel for his book, *The Case for a Creator,* there are thirty constants that are fine-tuned to a precise number and if any of them vary even insignificantly, earth would be a "waste place" as described in this passage.[12]

Fine-tuning demands a fine-tuner. This passage identifies Him unequivocally... And God fine-tuned it specifically for us, then charged us with its care (Genesis 1:27-30).

Lord God, it is quite a responsibility that You've given us. Your creation was perfect and our sin provoked a curse on it all, but Your promise is that it will be restored in You. Our hope is secure! Amen.

---

[11] Patrick Glynn, "The Making and Unmaking of an Atheist" in: *God: The Evidence* (Rocklin, CA: Forum, 1997), 1-20

[12] Lee Strobel, *The Case for a Creator* (Zondervan 2004) p. 128 – 152.

Genesis 1:11-12:
Then God said, "Let the earth sprout vegetation, plants yielding seed, and fruit trees on the earth bearing fruit after their kind with seed in them"; and it was so. The earth brought forth vegetation, plants yielding seed after their kind, and trees bearing fruit with seed in them, after their kind; and God saw that it was good.

This passage occurred on day three of creation. It contains the first three of ten instances where scripture uses the words "after their kind". These words are imperative in God's creation.

The MacArthur Study Bible comments on this passage:

God set in motion a providential process whereby the vegetable kingdom could reproduce through seeds which would maintain each one's unique characteristic.[13]

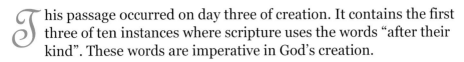

Not only were plants created "after their kind", God designed in them the capacity to reproduce in that way.

Notice that twice in this passage, Moses used the phrase "with seed in them". Not only were plants created "after their kind", God designed in them the capacity to reproduce in that way. This principle was extended to every living thing that God created, fish and birds on day five and land animals and humans on day six.

The existence of plants and trees are remarkably important to earth's ecosystem:
- They produce 50% of our oxygen.
- They provide habitats and food for animals.
- They help preserve soil by keeping it in place.
- They provide products for our consumption: fruits and vegetables to eat, wood for construction and cotton for clothes.

Just as animals and humans are dependent upon plants for survival, plants are dependent as well. They need the sun and the rain to grow as well as the rich soil. They need bees for pollination and underground creatures whose burrowing provides air in the soil for plant roots.

Our Creator has thought of everything. It is a truly a wondrous creation.

Thank You, Lord God for every living thing and for the way Your creation all works together to sustain life. You are most worthy of praise! Amen.

---

[13] The MacArthur Study Bible NASB Version, *Thomas Nelson Publishing, 2006.* Page 16

Psalm 65:9:
You visit the earth and cause it to overflow;
You greatly enrich it; The stream of God is full of water;
You prepare their grain, for thus You prepare the earth.

Scripture is filled with accounts of God's provision. Perhaps the most memorable occurred during the Exodus when God provided food for the Israelites with manna & quail (Exodus 16:1-21). He brought water from a rock at Meribah (Numbers 20:9-11) and turned bitter water sweet at Marah (Exodus 15:23-25).

This passage from the Psalms is beautiful in its simplicity but profound in its content. God has provided everything that we need for nourishment.

He prepared the earth: Soil serves as a platform from which the crops grow that feed us. It absorbs carbon dioxide, methane and water and recycles nutrients so that living things can use them over and over.

This passage from the Psalms is beautiful in its simplicity but profound in its content. God has provided everything that we need for nourishment.

He prepared the grain: Wheat, corn, rye, oats, rice and millet are all grains that we eat, and planting their seed will produce abundantly more. He provided liquid water, vibrant sunlight and the nutrients necessary to make it grow.

The earth overflows as well with fruit and vegetables.

Most trees grow to enormous heights: the oak, the sycamore, the pine... but fruit trees won't grow much higher than 18'. At that height they are easily accessible for us to gather the fruit and enjoy its sweetness.

Jesus said in Matthew 6:26: *"Look at the birds of the air, that they do not sow, nor reap nor gather into barns, and yet your heavenly Father feeds them. Are you not worth much more than they?"*

His bountiful and sustainable provision answer that question decisively.

Lord God, thank You that You are ever-mindful of us and have provided for all of our needs. All praise and honor are Yours. Amen.

Genesis 1:14:
Then God said, "Let there be lights in the firmament of the heavens to divide the day from the night; and let them be for signs and seasons, and for days and years;" (NKJV)

his verse is the beginning of God's description of day four of creation. Before He even tells us of the two great lights in the heavens (v.16-18), He tells us their two-fold purpose:

1. To divide the day from the night.
2. For signs and seasons, and for days and years.

The lights in the firmament serve as markers for us and they are instrumental in creating the seasons, which are determined by the position of the earth in relation to those two great lights.

How exactly are the seasons determined?

The earth rotates at a speed of 1,040 miles per hour at the equator, on an axis that is tilted at 23.5°. We are orbiting the sun at the incredible speed of 67,000 miles per hour and we will complete the circuit in one year.

As we move around the sun, the tilt is always in the same direction, so when we are on one side, the northern hemisphere is closer to the sun and when we are on the other side, the southern hemisphere is closer. This, along with the angle that the sunlight strikes the earth is the way that God creates the seasons. Because of the tilt, when it is summer in the northern hemisphere, it is winter in the southern, and vice-versa.

> *The lights in the firmament serve as markers for us and they are instrumental in creating the seasons, which are determined by the position of the earth in relation to those two great lights.*

Each season has its purpose in God's plan. Jeremiah 5:24 proclaims:

'They do not say in their heart, "Let us now fear the LORD our God, who gives rain in its season, both the autumn rain and the spring rain, who keeps for us the appointed weeks of the harvest."

We have seasons in our lives as well, Solomon tells us in Ecclesiastes 3:11 that God has made everything appropriate in its time and that He has set eternity in our hearts. Our highest calling is to serve Him.

Lord God, the changing of the seasons and their purpose in Your divine plan are one more reminder of Your wisdom and power. Let each season be a time of reflection for all who call on Your name. Amen.

Psalm 65:8:
They who dwell in the ends of the earth stand in awe of Your signs; You make the dawn and the sunset shout for joy.

*G*od's creation is not just a marvel of technology and wisdom. Neither is it just incomprehensible complexity and design. It is also magnificent beauty and incomparable splendor.

In this Psalm, David sets forth in awe:

"You make the dawn and the sunset shout for joy".

He is viewing the world as a tapestry of vibrant color and prolific artistry that could only have been initiated by divine ingenuity.

The word "joy" used in this passage is the imperfect tense of the Hebrew word *ranan,* which means "to give a ringing cry". The imperfect tense conveys that it is a continuing, or unfinished activity.

> *Effectively, what David is saying here is that God created the dawn and the sunset to give a never-ending ringing cry of joy… as the world turns, the sun is always rising or setting somewhere.*

Effectively, what David is saying here is that God created the dawn and the sunset to give a never-ending ringing cry of joy… as the world turns, the sun is always rising or setting somewhere.

It isn't just the dawn and sunset that exude dynamic color in God's composition. It is all around us. Rainbows, butterflies, flowers, peacock and parrot feathers and turning leaves in the fall are just a few that come to mind. Proponents of evolution are hard-pressed to explain the emergence of esthetic beauty by random processes.

It isn't just David that stands in awe. We do as well. David says *"They who dwell in the ends of the earth stand in awe."* Nowhere on this earth is so remote that God's transcendent artisanship can't be recognized and admired.

Lord God, thank You for creating a world of radiant beauty that is an ongoing reflection of the love that You have for us. Amen.

Genesis 1:16-18:
God made the two great lights, the greater light to
govern the day, and the lesser light to govern the night;
He made the stars also. God placed them in the expanse
of the heavens to give light on the earth, and to govern
the day and the night, and to separate the light from
the darkness; and God saw that it was good.

The sun and moon are both vital components of the remarkable symbiosis in God's creation. This passage of scripture is strikingly understated in regard to their importance. Yes, the sun and the moon provide light but they provide so much more.

All of life is dependent in some way on the energy produced by the sun. It provides warmth, its energy is critical for photosynthesis which turns the light energy into chemical energy necessary for the crops that provide us with food. Earth would be uninhabitable without the sun being in its exact location, 93 million miles away.

The moon is critical as well. It reflects the sun to light the night sky when the sun is on the other side of the earth. Just as the sun is in the perfect location, so is the moon, which is responsible for stabilizing the earth's rotation. It is the moon that controls the tides, which are responsible for oxygenating the waters and for regulating the ocean's currents. The tides also prevent the water from becoming stagnant. If the moon were a little closer to earth or a little further away, it would not provide this important function.

> The simple statement "He made the stars also" reflects a hugely significant reality… it is estimated that there are 200,000,000,000 stars in our galaxy alone.

The simple statement "He made the stars also" reflects a hugely significant reality… it is estimated that there are 200,000,000,000 stars in our galaxy alone. It is estimated that there are 170,000,000 galaxies in the known universe.

Isaiah 40:26 tells us that our all-knowing God calls them all by name.

The magi followed a star to find Jesus. Sailors and pilots have used the stars to navigate the earth. They are God's guideposts.

The power and glory of our God are on continuous display in the firmament!

Lord God, the vastness and beauty of the cosmos is mystifying. Your might and majesty are unfathomable. It is wondrous indeed that all of this was created with us in mind. Amen.

Jeremiah 10:12:
It is He who made the earth by His power,
Who established the world by His wisdom;
And by His understanding He has stretched out the heavens.

$\mathcal{T}$hose who espouse the Big Bang Theory are very certain of two things: The universe had a beginning and it is expanding.

As Bible-believing Christians, we would agree with both of those assessments, although we would diverge quite sharply from the rest of their thinking.

That the universe had a beginning is today a core belief of Big Bang theorists but as recently as the 1960's many believed in the "steady-state model", the idea that the universe does not change and that it is eternal. World-renowned cosmologist Carl Sagan was famous for saying "*The cosmos is all there is or was or ever will be*"[14]. There is indeed something eternal. It is the Creator God. (Psalm 90:2)

What now has considerable consensus in the world of science (that the universe had a beginning) was recorded by Moses thousands of years ago, in the very first verse of the bible: "*In the beginning, God made the heavens and the earth.*" It is interesting that Moses made no attempt to explain the concept of God or in any way to prove His existence. He states unequivocally that He is the Creator.

That the universe is expanding is their other central tenet and in fact, it is a key component of the Big Bang theory. Their observation is that galaxies are moving away from each other.

Scripture is resolute on this subject. Seventeen times the bible tells us that God "stretches out" the heavens, including today's passage in Jeremiah. Isaiah 40:22 tells us that He stretches out the heavens "like a curtain". In Isaiah 45:12 God says that not only did He stretch out the heavens, but that He ordained all their host.

17th Century Christian astronomer Johannes Kepler once said in reference to his work:

"*I was merely thinking God's thoughts after Him. Since we astronomers are priests of the highest God in regard to the book of nature, it benefits us to be thoughtful, not of the glory of our minds, but rather, above all else, of the glory of God.*".[15]

Lord, the heavens are an astounding reminder of Your creative genius. Scientific discoveries are nothing more than a recognition that a great mind went before us. All glory and honor to You. Amen.

---

[14] https://www.goodreads.com/quotes/178439-the-cosmos-is-all-that-is-or-was-or-ever
[15] https://www.newworldencyclopedia.org/entry/Johannes_Kepler

Psalm 19:1-2:
The heavens are telling of the glory of God; And their expanse is declaring the work of His hands. Day to day pours forth speech, And night to night reveals knowledge.

*R*eflection on the absolute immensity of the cosmos is a mind-boggling experience that proclaims the magnitude of the One who created it all.

The observable universe is 13.8 billion light years across, although estimates place the actual size at 19 billion light years. Exactly how big is that? A light year is 5.88 trillion miles, so the estimated size of the universe is:

111,720,000,000,000,000,000,000 miles across... and growing.
(111 billion, 720 million trillion miles)

If we were to believe those who posit the "Big Bang" theory, all of that matter and energy were once occupying an infinitely dense singularity that exploded about 13.7 billion years ago into the universe of order and complexity that we observe today.

Scripture, of course, tells a quite different story, one that David is recounting in this Psalm. The hand of God created it all... and He designed it in such a way that we can learn about His creativity and power.

> The hand of God created it all... and He designed it in such a way that we can learn about His creativity and power.

The earth's position in the universe is perfect in terms of discovering God's handiwork:

The Sun is about 400 times more distant than the moon. It is also about 400 times larger than the moon.

These two facts make it possible for us to observe a solar eclipse. By observing them, astronomers learn about the nature of stars. Observing them also enables astronomers to calculate the change in the earth's rotation over the past several thousand years and a solar eclipse in 1919 verified Einstein's theory of relativity by confirming that gravity bends light.

The more God reveals to us, the more humbled we become.

"For My hand made all these things, Thus all these things came into being," declares the LORD. "But to this one I will look, To him who is humble and contrite of spirit, and who trembles at My word." (Isaiah 66:2)

Lord, it is indeed humbling to view this universe and understand that it is us to whom You are mindful. We bow before You. Amen.

Genesis 1:20:
Then God said, "Let the waters teem with swarms of living creatures, and let birds fly above the earth in the open expanse of the heavens."

$\mathcal{T}$his was the fifth day.

It is interesting that in this passage, God does not say "Let the waters teem with fish". After all, it is not just fish that live in the water, there are mammals and at one time there were marine reptiles as well. They would have all been created with this command.

When we think of creatures that live in the water, though, we primarily think of fish... and they are uniquely designed for life in the water.

Mammals who live in the sea have to surface in order to breathe in oxygen in the same way as mammals that live on land. Fish use their gills to pull oxygen out of the water. They then exchange it for carbon dioxide just as we do and just as we expel the carbon dioxide through our nostrils, they have slits behind their gills for it to pass through. This is masterful design!

Created on the same day, their needs were so different, but an ever-mindful and creative God provided what they required.

Birds have an equally amazing respiratory system. Their metabolism is enormously high because of the amount of work they have to do in order to fly. Whereas mammals have a two-way bellows-type system (breathing in and out), God designed birds with a one-way flow-through system in which there is a continuous supply of fresh air entering their lungs. This design is optimized for light weight and efficiency, and ensures there is always a high concentration of oxygen in their blood which gives them the energy needed for flight.

Created on the same day, their needs were so different, but an ever-mindful and creative God provided what they required.

The Lord created His birds with great care and detail, but as He says in Luke 12:7: *"you are worth more than many sparrows."*

Lord God, Your works and creativity are truly awe-inspiring. As we contemplate the wonders of the animal kingdom it is a constant source of worshipful praise. Amen.

Genesis 1:24:
Then God said, "Let the earth bring forth living creatures after their kind: cattle and creeping things and beasts of the earth after their kind"; and it was so.

On the sixth day, prior to creating man, God created the land animals and creeping things "after their kind". That descriptive phrase is used ten times in the creation account in scripture. Its meaning is profound.

If this is the way that God created, then the theory of evolution can't be true and the fossil record bears that out. Dr. Jonathan Sarfati notes that:

> *Evolution cannot possibly explain these things… it can only be the hand of an all-powerful Creator.*

"…the fossil record shows that animals appear abruptly and fully formed, with only a handful of debatable examples of alleged transitional forms."[16]

God created "kinds" of animals that could breed together and reproduce. He also created genetic variability in each kind of creature. Geneticists now know, for example, that the "dog kind" can be traced back to a pair of wolf-like creatures. Today we have big dogs & little dogs, long-haired and short-haired dogs and pointy-eared and floppy-eared dogs. That variability was manifest in the original two dogs that God created and has been in the gene-pool ever since.

Design in the animal kingdom is as obvious as it is amazing.
- The camel has a transparent eyelid that allows him to keep going in a sandstorm.
- The river otter has extraordinarily dense fur that is water-repellent and allows him to dive for food even in the most extreme cold conditions… the freezing water never gets through to his skin to make him cold.
- The bombardier beetle has an elaborate defense mechanism that allows it to mix chemicals in an explosion chamber and aim and shoot hot gas ($212°F$) at predators.
- An elephant's trunk is so sensitive that he can pick up a single blade of grass

Evolution cannot possibly explain these things… it can only be the hand of an all-powerful Creator.

Lord God, it is undeniable that only You could have the wisdom and creativity to design and speak into existence these magnificent animals. You have made it evident to all. Amen.

---

[16] Jonathan Sarfati, *Refuting Evolution*, (Master Books 1999), p. 136

Job 12:7-10:
"But now ask the beasts, and let them teach you; And the birds of the heavens, and let them tell you. Or speak to the earth, and let it teach you; And let the fish of the sea declare to you. Who among all these does not know that the hand of the LORD has done this, in whose hand is the life of every living thing, And the breath of all mankind?"

$\mathcal{I}$n today's passage, Job uses the animal kingdom to illustrate the sovereignty of God over all that He has created and rightly so... animals provide us with amazing insights into God's workmanship.

Animals are equipped by God with the instincts and skills necessary for survival. The Megapode or "Incubator Bird" is a wonderful example of God's artistry and skillfulness.

Native to Australia, megapodes are unique in the way that they incubate their eggs. The process is fascinating.

> *Animals are equipped by God with the instincts and skills necessary for survival.*

The male builds a nest that to you and I would look like an enormous brush pile. It is dug into the ground about 3', piled as high as 15' and spread out as much as 50'. Inside the nest, the male has provided a fermenting compost that will produce the heat necessary for incubation.

The female, after making sure that the nest is suitable, will then lay as many as 35 eggs and leave the nest. It is up to the male to maintain a precise temperature of 91° F and a humidity of 99.5% in the nest while still making sure that the chicks have enough air to breathe. There are thousands of tiny holes in the egg shell to allow the air to get through to the chick.

The male can be seen adding material to and subtracting it from the pile, digging cone-shaped holes to get more moisture down into the nest and somehow maintaining temperature and humidity inside the nest with only the slightest variance. Once the eggs are hatched, it takes about three days for the chicks to dig their way out and then they are on their own. Neither the mother nor the father stays around to feed them or teach them how to "build the pile". When the time comes, they will do that innately.

How does the male know how to compost? How does he know the precise temperature and humidity necessary inside the nest? Where did he develop the skill to maintain them both at the proper levels? How do the chicks know how to do this with no instruction?

It is, of course, the hand of the Lord that has done this.

Lord God, how can anyone deny that it is Your wisdom and creativity on display in the animal kingdom? The more we learn, the more we are speechless before You. Amen.

Colossians 2:8:
See to it that no one takes you captive
through philosophy and empty deception,
according to the tradition of men, according
to the elementary principles of the world,
rather than according to Christ.

$\mathcal{P}$aul's warning to the Colossians is as appropriate today as it was then. Four terms stand out in Paul's warning:

1. Philosophy
2. Empty Deception
3. Tradition of Men
4. Principles of the World

A philosophy, by definition is a set of principles which inform a system of thought. If the system of thought, or worldview, is based on a false premise, then all philosophical reasoning based on that premise falls apart.

The theory of evolution is such a philosophy. While many of its proponents

> God is unequivocal about the way He created. Ten times in Genesis 1 He tells us that He created everything "after their kind".

profess it to be a "proven fact" it is no such thing. In reality, it cannot be verified nor can it be falsified by scientific testing. It is nothing more than materialistic philosophy.

The Scientific Method was developed to take bias out of the process. It starts with a hypothesis, then development of a test to determine the accuracy of the hypothesis. The test is designed to prove the hypothesis to be true or false.

There is no conceivable way to test the theory of evolution in order to verify or disprove its construct. Belief in it is a philosophy and to put it in Paul's terms, it is based on the elementary principles of the world and the tradition of men... and it is the epitome of empty deception.

God is unequivocal about the way He created. Ten times in Genesis He tells us that He created everything "after their kind". This, by itself, eliminates evolution as a possibility.

In today's verse, Paul tells us with clarity what we should avoid. He tells us with the same clarity who to embrace: Jesus Christ. The One who created us. The One who saved us. The One who will return to us and will abide with us in the heavenly kingdom. We place our trust, our hope and our eternal future in Him and Him alone.

Lord God, please guard us from philosophies and concepts that draw us away from You. Lead us always back to scripture in order to separate truth from error. Amen.

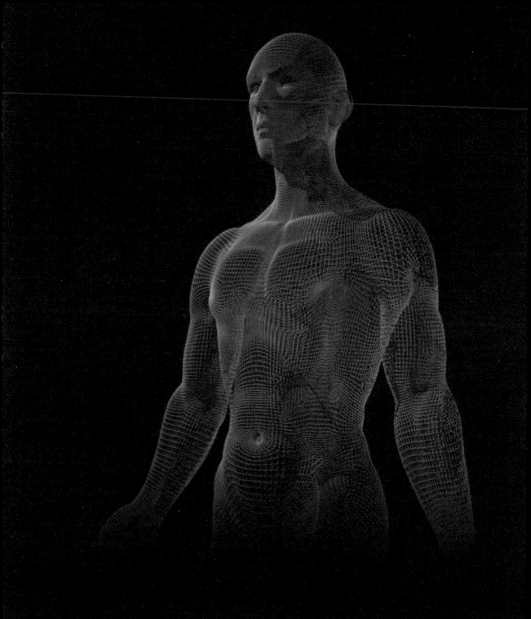

Genesis 1:26-27:
Then God said, "Let Us make man in Our image, according to Our likeness; and let them rule over the fish of the sea and over the birds of the sky and over the cattle and over all the earth, and over every creeping thing that creeps on the earth." God created man in His own image, in the image of God He created him; male and female He created them.

*T*oday's verses are filled with wonderful theology. It is the first indication scripture gives us that there is a triune God. They tell us that humanity bears the image of God and that God put us in charge of all that He created.

What exactly does it mean that we are created in God's image? It means that we are the centerpiece of all of creation. While God does not share His Divine attributes with us, He has shared with us his communicable attributes: We have intellect, we are able to reason, we have emotion and volitional will.

> *What exactly does it mean that we are created in God's image? It means that we are the centerpiece of all of creation.*

Unlike God, we do not make perfect use of these attributes but all of scripture testifies to our lofty place in God's creation:

- The Son of God was inserted into history for our benefit (1 John 4:9)
- Jesus endured excruciating punishment for us (Isaiah 53:5)
- Our inheritance is eternity with God (Titus 3:7)
- Our inheritance is secured through faith (2 Peter 1:3-5)

Scripture even tells us in Revelation 21 & 22 what that inheritance will look like... God will dwell among his people and all things will be made new. Those who overcome this world through the sacrifice of the Messiah will experience the entirety of the new creation, which will not include a physical temple.

Revelation 21:22 says:
I saw no temple in it, for the Lord God the Almighty and the Lamb are its temple.

When you are in the unending presence of God, such a building is unnecessary.

God Almighty, it is humbling to realize that this beautiful creation was brought into existence for us. You have given us dominion over all of it. Please help us to live our lives with that thought in mind and to wisely care for it. Amen.

Genesis 1:28-29:
And God blessed them; and God said to them, "Be fruitful
and multiply, and fill the earth, and subdue it; and rule over
the fish of the sea and over the birds of the sky, and over
every living thing that moves on the earth." Then God said,
"Behold, I have given you every plant yielding seed that is
on the surface of all the earth, and every tree which has fruit
yielding seed; it shall be food for you;"

This completed God's creative activity. He had created it all through His Son and He would now put man in charge of all that He had made. He had given us His communicable attributes: intellect, emotion, volitional will and the ability to reason. He had therefore equipped us with everything that we needed to have command over all He had created. God's creation was not only incredibly beautiful, it was orderly and ready for us to step in.

This passage shows four commands that He gave to Adam and Eve (and to us as well):

1. Be fruitful and multiply.
2. Fill the earth.
3. Subdue the earth.
4. Rule over every living thing.

Humanity has in large part been diligent in following these commands, although filling the earth required a little prompting by God at the Tower of Babel (Genesis 11:1-8)

> He had therefore equipped us with everything that we needed to have command over all He had created.

The Hebrew word for subdue is *kabash* which literally means to "bring into bondage". As our knowledge increases and we look at the advances made in farming technology, mining and scientific discovery, we have truly taken advantage of earth's boundless treasures. God has genuinely blessed us and in many ways, we have subdued the physical earth.

We have asserted dominance over the animal kingdom as well.

The passage closes with God giving us every seed-bearing plant to eat. It would be after the flood, some 2,000 years later, that God would give permission for man to eat meat (Genesis 9:3).

We were endowed and equipped by God to accomplish what He had called us to do physically.

He equipped us spiritually as well... that was a completely different matter.

Thank You Lord that You didn't just command these things but You gave us the skill and ability required to fulfill them. Amen.

Genesis 2:7:
Then the LORD God formed man of dust from the ground,
and breathed into his nostrils the breath of life; and man
became a living being.

God had told us of man's creation in Genesis 1:27. Today's passage fills in the details on exactly how God accomplished it. Adam was formed from the dust of the ground, in fact his very name comes from the Hebrew word *adâmah,* which means "cultivated ground".

It is interesting that Adam's name is not mentioned at all until Genesis 2:20 when he himself named the animals that God brought to him.

The second part of this verse will be our focal point. After God had formed him, there was still no life until God breathed it into Adam. The breath of God initiated his human life and all human life.

Biogenesis is a law of nature that is very simple in its construct: Life only comes from preexisting life.

In regard to life, proponents of the theory of evolution are put in the untenable position of defending a belief that is antithetical to what is observed.

Dr. Werner Gitt, a PhD engineer, wrote this concerning natural law:

Laws of nature describe events, phenomena and occurrences that consistently and repeatedly take place. They are thus universally valid laws... Due to their explanatory power, laws of nature enjoy the highest level of confidence in science.[17]

Biogenesis is a law of nature that is very simple in its construct: Life only comes from preexisting life.

In the world of science, a law of nature can have no known violations. Life, then, has never been observed to come from anything inorganic (non-life) as posited by the theory of evolution.

If by natural processes life can only come from preexisting life, then first life was necessarily ordained by something completely outside of nature. As Christians, we trust in the Word of God which tells us that it was the breath of God.

Lord God, we owe our very lives to You. Thank You for communicating your principles for godliness to us in scripture. Give us the strength to live our lives in submission to them. Amen.

---

[17] Scientific laws of information and their implications—part 1 by Werner Gitt
http://creation.com/laws-of-information-1

Isaiah 66:1-2:
"Heaven is My throne and the earth is My footstool.
Where then is a house you could build for Me?
And where is a place that I may rest?
For My hand made all these things,
Thus all these things came into being," declares the LORD.
"But to this one I will look, to him who is humble and
contrite of spirit, and who trembles at My word."

The God who made everything needs not a place to dwell. Isaiah's imagery here is superb, God's throne is in heaven and the earth is His footstool. In other words, the entire universe belongs to Him. He created it and since He is omnipresent, the entire universe is where he dwells.

Scripture describes God walking in the Garden of Eden (Genesis 3:8). It also describes His presence in the tabernacle (Exodus 40:34) and in the temple built by Solomon (1 Kings 8:10-11).

When He was here on earth, Jesus was physically present in the second temple. In fact, He told the apostles of its coming destruction (Matthew 24:2).

Yet God asks this question through Isaiah: "Where is a place that I may rest?" He answers the question Himself... It is His desire to dwell in us. He is looking for those of us who are humble, contrite of spirit and who tremble at His word.

> *It is a marvelous truth that when we submit to the Lordship of Christ, we become a temple for Father, Son & Holy Spirit and they are unshakably and enduringly ours!*

He chooses us over everything else in all of creation. How's that for a humbling thought? John 14:23 quotes Jesus: *"If anyone loves Me, he will keep My word; and My Father will love him, and We will come to him and make Our abode with him."*

The Greek word for abode (*monē*) is used only twice in the new testament, both times are by Jesus and both times in John 14 (14:2, 23). It conveys the idea of permanence and of security.

It is a marvelous truth that when we submit to the Lordship of Christ, we become a temple for Father, Son & Holy Spirit and they are unshakably and enduringly ours!

Lord, we are truly unworthy of You. It is a wonderful blessing to know that we are securely in Your loving arms. Amen.

Ephesians 2:10:
For we are His workmanship,
created in Christ Jesus for good
works, which God prepared
beforehand so that we would
walk in them.

orkmanship as defined by dictionary.com[18]:

1. The art or skill of a workman or workwoman.
2. The quality or mode of execution, as of a thing made.
3. The product or result of labor and skill; work executed.

We are God's workmanship, in fact, we are the pinnacle of creation and as such God gave us dominion over it all. We are His representatives here on earth. That defines our special relationship with the Creator and this passage tells us that part of that responsibility is to fulfill the good works that God has prepared for us beforehand.

These good works are not a means to our salvation, they are evidence to an unbelieving world that we belong to Christ and they have been entrusted to us by the Father.

> These good works are not a means to our salvation, they are evidence to an unbelieving world that we belong to Christ and they have been entrusted to us by the Father.

We glorify God by showing His love to others through the good works that God has prepared for us.

John 13 gives us a vivid picture of what that looks like.

People living in Jerusalem in the first century traveled everywhere by foot. They walked on dirt roads in intensely hot weather while wearing sandals. When they arrived at their destination their feet were disgusting to say the least.

In society at that time, foot-washing was assigned to slaves that were of the lowest in rank. Yet, at the Last Supper, Jesus Christ, the Son of God and Messiah condescended to wash the feet of the Apostles. By performing this selfless act, Jesus modeled the love and humility that as followers of Christ we should exhibit to the world.

Of course, nothing compares to the love and humility that was exemplified by Jesus' death on the cross.

Modeling Christ to a hostile and unbelieving world is our highest calling.

Lord God help us to exemplify Christ in this world and to be willing servants in recognizing and carrying out the good works that You have prepared for us. Amen.

[18] https://www.dictionary.com/browse/workmanship?s=t

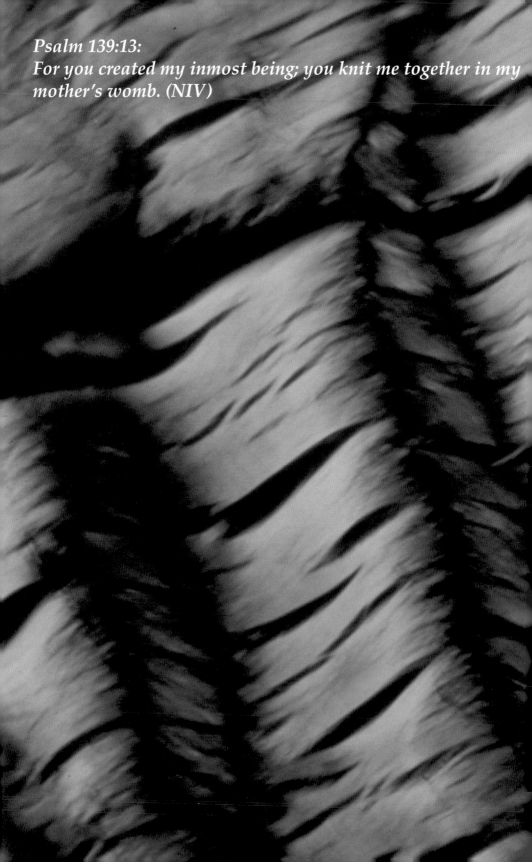

Psalm 139:13:
For you created my inmost being; you knit me together in my mother's womb. (NIV)

This Psalm of David is a worshipful song of praise in recognition of God's omniscience.

In verse 2 he says *"you know my thoughts from afar"*. In verse 3 he says *"you are intimately acquainted with all my ways"*. In verse 4 he says *"Behold, O LORD, You know it all"*. Indeed, David recognizes that God knows everything about him.

In verses 13-16, he praises the creator God, who made him and watched over him while he was yet unborn.

When David used the phrase "you knit me together" it was a judicious choice of words. What the NIV (and also the ESV) translates as "knit" is the Hebrew word *sakak* which means "to entwine". The NASB translates it as "wove". These words convey the idea of material being interlaced to form a durable finished product.

> *When collagen is viewed under a microscope, it is abundantly clear that David could not have described it any more precisely than he did in this passage of scripture.*

Collagen is a protein that exists outside the cell and it is a key structural component in the skin, bone, cartilage, tendons, lung tissue and blood vessels serving to connect the tissue between our cells.

- It is the most abundant protein in our bodies
- It makes up 75% of the dry weight of skin.
- It gives the skin flexibility, resilience and strength.
- It is considered the glue that holds the body together.
- It provides structure and firmness.

When collagen is viewed under a microscope (see picture at left), it is abundantly clear that David could not have described it any more precisely than he did in this passage of scripture.

In verse 14, David says that we are fearfully and wonderfully made. Amen, David.

Lord God, truly You know us intimately and completely. We are thankful for Your affection and for the mercy and grace that You bestow on us every day. Amen.

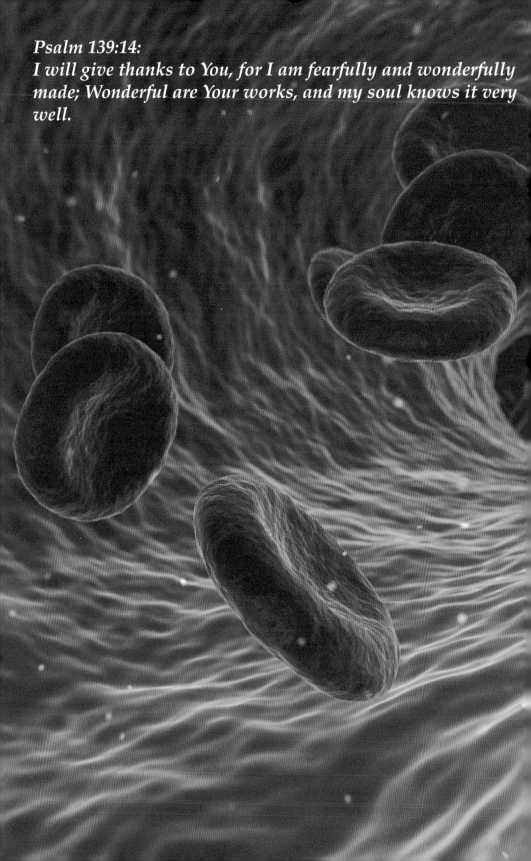

Psalm 139:14:
I will give thanks to You, for I am fearfully and wonderfully
made; Wonderful are Your works, and my soul knows it very
well.

*F*earfully and wonderfully made... how remarkably descriptive. God's majesty and power can be seen in the intricacy and detail found in every human. Life can only have been divinely ordained.

Consider the extraordinary complexity of our circulatory system:

The human heart beats 72 times every minute, 100,000 beats per day pumping the equivalent of 2,000 gallons of blood through the 60,000 miles of blood vessels in our bodies. The blood transports food, water and oxygen through our blood vessels to our organs and tissues.

> *The human heart beats 72 times per minute, 100,000 beats per day pumping the equivalent of 2,000 gallons of blood through the 60,000 miles of blood vessels in our bodies.*

The circulatory system is comprised of the heart, left and right ventricles, lungs, pulmonary veins & pulmonary arteries, aorta, arteries, capillaries and veins, which must work together to sustain life. It is a marvelously complex machine but without hemoglobin to carry oxygen through our blood vessels to our organs and tissues, it still wouldn't be sufficient for life to exist.

How complex is hemoglobin? It is comprised of four chains of amino acids, two identical "alpha" chains containing 141 and two identical "beta" chains containing 146 for a total of 574. The theory of evolution posits that this came about randomly over eons of time. The probability of getting just one alpha and one beta chain (remember, there are two of each) by random processes is one chance in 2.5×10^{373}. It is unreasonable in the extreme to believe that this is even remotely possible.

Scripture speaks a lot about the human heart but not in physical terms.

Ecclesiastes 3:11 says:

He has made everything beautiful in its time. Also, He has put eternity in their hearts, except that no one can find out the work that God does from beginning to end. (NKJV)

God created us with an eternal purpose in mind. Our innermost thoughts and passions should be a reflection of the gracious and merciful God who made us.

Truly, Lord God, we cannot even begin to fathom the miracle of life and the work that You do from beginning to end. We are in awe of Your wisdom and power. We are truly "fearfully and wonderfully made" and we marvel at Your works. Amen.

Acts 17:26:
And He has made from one blood every nation of men to dwell on all the face of the earth, and has determined their preappointed times and the boundaries of their dwellings (NKJV)

This passage is unequivocal. We are all "one blood". We are not just brothers and sisters in Christ, we are brothers and sisters by blood and can all trace our lineage back through Noah and his sons to Adam.

Regardless of physical differences, cultural differences or personal biases, the "brotherhood of man" is not just a platitude, it is a fact that scripture clearly reveals to us. The bible is also clear that we are sinners in need of redemption:

> *Regardless of physical differences or personal biases, the "brotherhood of man" is not just a platitude, it is a fact that scripture has clearly revealed to us.*

- We are created in God's image. (Gen 1:27)
- We are "one blood" (Acts 17:26)
- Sin entered the world through Adam and it affected all of mankind. (Romans 5:12)
- The One who redeemed us of that sin had to be human. (Galatians 4:4-5, Hebrews 2:10-11)
- Jesus, the Son of God was sent to earth to repair the damage done by sin. (1 John 3:8)
- Jesus' lineage is traced back to Adam (Luke 3:23-38)
- Death is a temporary consequence of sin. (1 Corinthians 15:22)
- We received our earthly body through Adam, our resurrected (spiritual) body will come through Jesus Christ. (1 Corinthians 15:45)
- Our only requirement is to trust in Christ's sacrifice. (Romans 10:9)
- Our eternal inheritance is secure. (1 Peter 1:3-5)

We are truly one blood. More importantly, as Christian brothers and sisters we are bound by another blood. The blood of the lamb, the Son of God, the perfect sacrifice that the Father sent to atone for our sins and confer on us the only righteousness that will gain us eternity with our Creator and Savior. Blood shed on the cross. Blood that covers our iniquity. Blood that once and forever washes us clean so that in the eyes of God we are worthy to be in His presence. For eternity. Hallelujah!

Thank You, Jesus for the incredible sacrifice that You made on our behalf. Thank You for the awesome inheritance that awaits us and for eternity in Your presence. Amen.

Psalm 8:3-5:
When I consider Your heavens, the work of Your fingers, the moon and the stars, which You have ordained; What is man that You take thought of him, And the son of man that You care for him? Yet You have made him a little lower than God, And You crown him with glory and majesty!

*I*n today's passage, David expresses his astonishment that God would esteem man to such a degree. After all, man is but an insignificant speck when compared to the immensity of the universe that God created. He asks the question: *"What is man that You take thought of him, And the son of man that You care for him?"*

It is of great significance that God created man in His image and likeness (Genesis 1:26-27). David uses the phrase *"You made him a little lower than God"* to make that point. Man is defined by his superiority in all of creation and by the fact that God put him in charge of it all. That is emblematic of how God thinks of him and why He cares for him.

> *In all of creation, we are the only ones that can be restored to a right relationship with our holy God. Fallen angels have not been given that luxury.*

How much so? Scripture documents a historical narrative of creation, sin, repentance, mercy, grace, redemption and ultimately, a restoration of the original perfect creation. Jesus Christ is the focal point of all of this. He left the glory of heaven and His seat at the right hand of the Father to submit to His will and be inserted into history, the perfect lamb needed for the perfect sacrifice that would redeem those of us who put our faith in Him.

How much so? In all of creation, we are the only ones that can be restored to a right relationship with our holy God. Fallen angels have not been given that luxury.

Jude 6 tells us:
And angels who did not keep their own domain, but abandoned their proper abode, He has kept in eternal bonds under darkness for the judgment of the great day.

Repentance is not theirs to offer God. It is only ours. It is too late for them to submit to the Lordship of Christ. As long as we have breath, it is never too late for us.

Lord God, how mindful You are of us. We are humbled beyond words and pray for friends and family that do not know You. Please bless them today with the gift of salvation. Amen.

Matthew 19:4-5:
And He answered and said to them, "Have you not read that He who made them at the beginning 'made them male and female,' and said, 'For this reason a man shall leave his father and mother and be joined to his wife, and the two shall become one flesh'?" (NKJV)

his was Jesus' response to Pharisees who had confronted Him about divorce. These short two verses are full of theology.

First and foremost, we know that God the Father created all things through His Son, Jesus, (John 1:3,10, 1 Corinthians 8:6. Colossians 1:16, Hebrews 1:2) so when Jesus refers to "He who made them", He's talking about Himself. Who would know better than He about the creation? Not only how and why it was accomplished but also very importantly, when it was accomplished.

Who would know better than He about the creation? Not only how and why it was accomplished but also very importantly, when it was accomplished.

Jesus was the "who", so in telling the "when", He is speaking with the authority of the One who carried it out. He tells the Pharisees that He made male and female "at the beginning". These words from Jesus should put an end to the idea of evolution for any Christian.

Proponents of the theory of evolution propose a time frame of billions of years (in reality, not nearly enough time), yet the One who did the actual creating says that male and female were created "at the beginning". If evolution were true, we would have emerged near the end.

Scripture also tells us that we are created in the image of God. Evolutionists say that chemicals somehow coalesced to form a gene in a "warm little pond". Is that the image of God?

This passage ends with Jesus quoting from Genesis 2:24, in that passage God established the very first human institution, marriage, a subject about which scripture has quite a lot to say. In fact, marriage is used as a metaphor for Christ's relationship with the church. (2Corinthians 11:2. Ephesians 5:22-24, Revelation 21:9)

We will be joined together for eternity with the One who created us and came to earth, God in human form, to rescue us. Our hope is secure in Christ.

Lord God, You have made it obvious that we are created beings. As such we are answerable to our Creator. Give us the strength to live our lives in submission to You. Amen.

Genesis 2:16-17:
And the LORD God commanded the man, saying, "Of every tree of the garden you may freely eat; but of the tree of the knowledge of good and evil you shall not eat, for in the day that you eat of it you shall surely die." (NKJV)

$\mathcal{G}$od's creation was perfect. At the end of the sixth day, when the creation was complete, He called it "very good".

The trials and tribulations of the world in which we live today can all be traced back to today's passage.

Scripture gives us no indication of God's purpose for prohibiting this tree in the garden, perhaps it was a test, but Adam knew that the consequence was death and he was at Eve's side when she ate. He took a bite as well. (Genesis 3:6)

> *Those thorns that were part of the curse were symbolically on the head of Jesus Christ when he died on the cross.*

Adam and Eve's submission to Satan's temptation and violation of this command resulted in the sin-cursed world in which we live today. Adam's failure to obey became our failure.

Genesis 3:16-20 describes the curse in detail. For the woman: Pain in childbirth and submission to her husband. For the man: Toil to produce food from the earth which would reluctantly yield its bounty. Thorns and thistles would make that labor more difficult. And of course, physical death is the primary consequence, just as God had promised.

Those thorns that were part of the curse were symbolically on the head of Jesus Christ when he died on the cross. Jesus bore the weight of that curse for us all and because of his sacrifice, the curse will one day be removed.

Revelation 22:1-3: *And he showed me a river of the water of life, clear as crystal, coming from the throne of God and of the Lamb, in the middle of its street. On either side of the river was the tree of life, bearing twelve kinds of fruit, yielding its fruit every month; and the leaves of the tree were for the healing of the nations. There will no longer be any curse; and the throne of God and of the Lamb will be in it, and His bond-servants will serve Him;*

The tree of prohibition will be replaced by trees of life and there will be no curse in the New Heaven and the New Earth

In this we can have immeasurable confidence, God sent his Son to undo the works of the devil (1 John 3:8) and to open the gates of the Kingdom to us. We will be with God for eternity.

Lord God we look forward to our future in the Kingdom where there will be no pain or suffering and eternity in Your presence is ours. Amen.

Job 38:4-6:
"Where were you when I laid the foundation of the earth? Tell Me, if you have understanding, Who set its measurements? Since you know. Or who stretched the line on it? "On what were its bases sunk? Or who laid its cornerstone"

C hapters 1 & 2 of the Book of Job record the catastrophic loss of his family and all of his possessions. He subsequently received advice from his three friends Eliphaz, Bildad and Zophar. Their dialogue was recorded beginning in Chapter 3 and running through the end of Chapter 31 at which time Elihu gave his assessment. At that point God had heard enough.

Chapters 38-41 record God's amazing response to Job making it clear that his friends did not know the mind of, nor did they speak for the Almighty. These four chapters are all about what He created and His wisdom, His power and sovereignty over it all. God leaves nothing to the imagination, He and only He is responsible for the cosmos, for nature and all of its intricacies and for the animals and their instincts. Every part of what He created is subservient to His will. Here are just a few of those mentioned in these chapters of Job:

He and only He is responsible for the cosmos, for nature and all of its intricacies and for the animals and their instincts.

- He made the dawn know its place (38:12)
- He makes the seeds of grass sprout (38:27)
- He established the laws of the universe (38:33)
- At His command the eagle and the hawk soar (39:26-27)

Job responds in 40:4:

"Behold, I am insignificant; what can I reply to You? I lay my hand on my mouth."

In 42:2-6 Job retracts and repents.

It is overwhelming to diligently look at God's stunning handiwork and consider the depth of His wisdom in creating it all.

Psalm 46:10 instructs us to *"be still and know that I am God"* and that *"He will be exalted among the nations and in the earth."*

Like Job, we are overwhelmed.

Lord God, we do exalt You. We, like Job, are insignificant. We are not, though, insignificant in Your eyes, for You created it all for us. Your Name is to be praised. Amen.

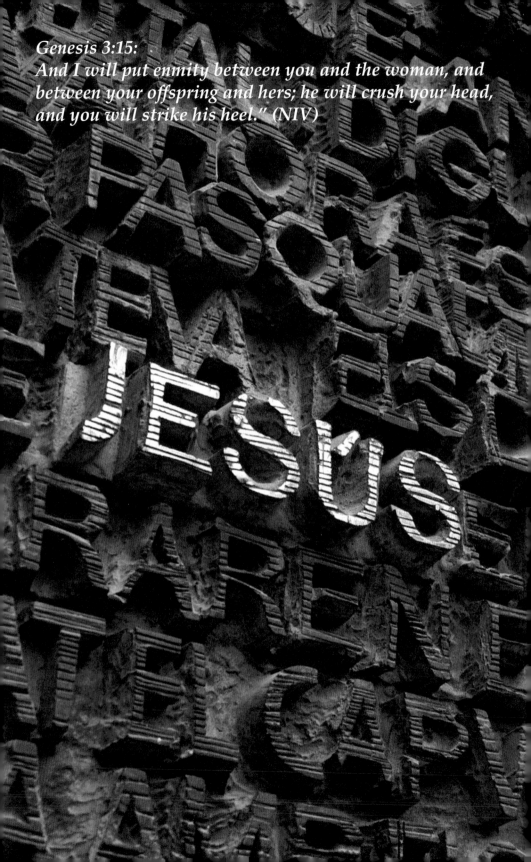

Genesis 3:15:
And I will put enmity between you and the woman, and
between your offspring and hers; he will crush your head,
and you will strike his heel." (NIV)

Theologians call today's passage the *Protoevangelium*, as it is the first indication given in scripture that there is a Messiah coming.

Adam and Eve had succumbed to the serpent's temptation and God is revealing to Satan what the future will bring... hostility between he and Eve and most strikingly, between his offspring and hers.

Satan's offspring are best described by Jesus in John 8:44. He is speaking to Jews who wish to kill him:

"You are of your father the devil, and you want to do the desires of your father. He was a murderer from the beginning, and does not stand in the truth because there is no truth in him. Whenever he speaks a lie, he speaks from his own nature, for he is a liar and the father of lies."

> **The cross of Christ is the power that is required to blunt the schemes of the devil, remove his tyranny in our lives and destroy all of his works.**

God tells Satan that Eve's offspring will crush his head, while Satan will only strike his heel. Eve's offspring can only be Jesus Christ. God is informing Satan that He is going to send someone to repair the contamination that Satan caused to His perfect creation. While Satan will cause Him to suffer (strike His heel), the death blow will belong to his adversary, the one whom God is sending.

Paul uses similar imagery in Romans 16:20: *The God of peace will soon crush Satan under your feet.*

Notice that Paul has added a third party to the equation. He advises followers of Christ that Satan will be crushed under their feet. Because of Christ's death and resurrection, we are participants with Him in the vanquishing of Satan, he is powerless against us (Hebrews 2:14).

Paul admonishes us to put on the full armor of God (Ephesians 6:11-13).

The cross of Christ is the power that is required to blunt the schemes of the devil, remove his tyranny in our lives and destroy all of his works.

The one who practices sin is of the devil; for the devil has sinned from the beginning. The Son of God appeared for this purpose, to destroy the works of the devil. (1 John 3:8)

Jesus Christ has vanquished Satan on our behalf. Ours is to trust and obey.

Thank You, Jesus for laying Your divinity aside in order to rescue us from the grasp of the devil and to secure our inheritance in heaven. Amen.

1 Corinthians 15:45:
So also it is written, "The first man, Adam, became a living soul." The last Adam became a life-giving spirit.

When we contemplate our Messiah and the incredible sacrifice that He made on our behalf, it is an inescapable truth that without the fall of man, His excruciating death and subsequent resurrection would have been unnecessary.

Had Adam and Eve not succumbed to Satan's temptation, the bible would have told a completely different story.

Romans 5:12 tells us: *"Therefore, just as through one man sin entered into the world, and death through sin, and so death spread to all men, because all sinned—"*

1 John 3:8 tells us: *"the one who practices sin is of the devil; for the devil has sinned from the beginning. The Son of God appeared for this purpose, to destroy the works of the devil."*

The first Adam brought sin, the second Adam (Jesus Christ) came to destroy it.

> *When we look at today's passage it becomes obvious that both the first and second Adam are essential to the Gospel message. One brought us death, the other eternal life!*

When we look at today's passage it becomes obvious that both the first and second Adam are essential to the Gospel message. One brought us death, the other eternal life!

Through the first Adam, we received our human bodies. We also became subject to death and all of the earthly consequences of the fall.

The merciful act of the second Adam acquired for us the righteousness to spend eternity in Paradise (Romans 4:23-25). Through the second Adam we will receive our spiritual bodies in the resurrection.

It is interesting that in this passage, Paul uses the term "living" in his description of the first Adam. He uses the word "life-giving" when referring to Jesus, the second Adam.

Jesus truly bestowed life on that which was dead.

Thank You Jesus for rescuing us and for presenting us with the everlasting life that we could never have earned on our own. We receive it with reverence and awe! Amen.

Genesis 2:2:
By the seventh day God completed His work which He had done, and He rested on the seventh day from all His work which He had done.

t the end of the sixth day, God had completed His work. He had created all things "both visible and invisible" (Colossians 1:16) and He had declared in Genesis 1:31 that it was "very good".

Laws of nature, done. Creation of matter, done. Energy and its sources, done. Life of all kinds, plant, animal and human, created with the ability to multiply. It was all done.

In other words, as this passage says: *"By the seventh day God completed His work"*.

Observable science and the laws of nature quite demonstrably support that creation is finished.

> *Natural processes cannot create or destroy energy nor can they create or destroy matter.*

The First Law of Thermodynamics states that energy cannot be created or destroyed by natural processes, although it can change form.

The Second Law of Thermodynamics states that the amount of usable energy in the universe is running out. In other words, energy is constantly being converted from a usable to an unusable state. There was a fixed amount of energy in the beginning and it is slowly being used up.

The Law of the Conservation of Matter states that the amount of matter in the universe is constant. By natural processes, it cannot be created or destroyed, although it too can change form.

The Law of Biogenesis states that life can only come from preexisting life.

Natural processes cannot create or destroy energy nor can they create or destroy matter. Nature, therefore, cannot be responsible for, nor can it explain the existence of either. Both had to have been ordained from outside of nature and there is a fixed amount of each.

First life had to be ordained from outside of nature as well, and it can only proliferate after its kind.

The writer of Hebrews tells us in Chapter 4:3:
"His works were finished from the foundation of the world".

Observable science and the laws of nature agree.

Lord God, it all points back to You and Your preeminence over everything that You created. Your works are a testament to Your sovereign will. Amen.

Genesis 2:3:
Then God blessed
the seventh day and
sanctified it, because in
it He rested from all His
work which God had
created and made.

God sanctified the seventh day... as Christians we know that means that He set it apart. He did this in the beginning, way before there was a Mosaic Law and way before there were any covenants between God and man.

God rested on the seventh day, modeling for us what would be our work cycle and the need for a day of rest. While God obviously has no need of rest, this passage is His affirmation that it is requisite for man.

> *God rested on the seventh day, modeling for us what would be our work cycle and the need for a day of rest.*

Scripture also tells us that the land requires rest. The Israelites were instructed that there was to be no sowing or reaping in the seventh year allowing the soil to be reinvigorated with necessary nutrients for the crops (Leviticus 25:1-7)

When God sanctified the seventh day, He also set it apart for worship. This was later codified by Moses with the fourth of the Ten Commandments.

Consider that on our calendars there are days, weeks, months and years. A day is one rotation of the earth on its axis. A month is one rotation of the moon around the earth and a year is one rotation of the earth around the sun... all are dictated by astronomy.

There is nothing astronomical about the seven-day week. From where did it come? Obviously, it can be traced back to this passage of scripture.

Various cultures have tried to change God's pattern over the centuries but to no avail. The ancient Egyptians experimented with ten-day weeks but when the Babylonians became dominant in the 6th Century BC, it was changed back to seven.

The Russians were the most recent culture to try to change it. In 1929 they went to 72 weeks of five days but they couldn't make it work, so in 1931 they went to a six-day week. That proved to be too chaotic as well and in 1940 they gave up and went back to God's standard.

What God set in motion at the beginning is the pattern we follow today... His will cannot be thwarted.

Lord God, this is a great reminder that You are sovereign over all. What You ordain will not be circumvented or defeated. Your command is supreme. Amen.

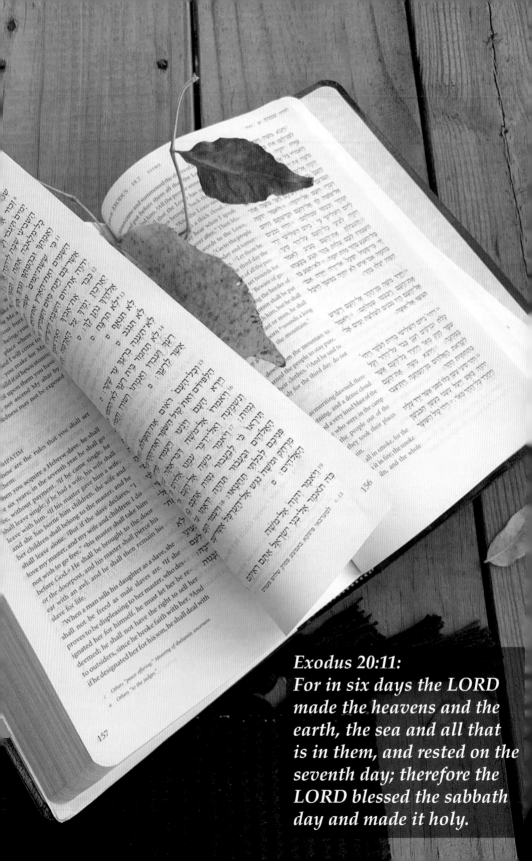

Exodus 20:11:
For in six days the LORD made the heavens and the earth, the sea and all that is in them, and rested on the seventh day; therefore the LORD blessed the sabbath day and made it holy.

There are only two of the ten commandments in which God gave Moses (and us) the reason for the commandment. One is the second commandment (Exodus 20:4-5):

"You shall not make for yourself an idol, or any likeness of what is in heaven above or on the earth beneath or in the water under the earth. You shall not worship them or serve them; for I, the LORD your God, am a jealous God, visiting the iniquity of the fathers on the children, on the third and the fourth generations of those who hate Me.

The other is in today's passage. He created in six days and rested on the seventh in order to create the Sabbath, a day set apart for rest and for worship of our Creator.

The Hebrew word for day is "Yom". It can mean a period of time when the sun is out (Genesis 1:14), it can mean an extended time period (Genesis 2:4) or it can be a 24-hour time period that requires a light source and one rotation of the earth on its axis (Genesis 1:5, 8, 13, 19, 23, 31).

> *He created in six days and rested on the seventh in order to create the Sabbath, a day set apart for rest and for worship of our Creator.*

An All-powerful God could have created everything in the blink of an eye... but He didn't. He intentionally took six days and He had Moses give us the details of each day of creation.

In fact, to ensure that we understand that these were 24-hour days, Moses ends each creation day with the phrase *"There was evening and there was morning"* followed by a number modifier that identifies the day that it happened.

The context couldn't be more obvious... God was setting the precedent for six days of work and one day of rest, a sanctified day that belongs to Him.

Lord God, it is a daily devotional to observe Your glorious handiwork. Thank You for giving us a day of reflection and worship to contemplate Your holiness and to grow ever closer to You. Amen.

Ecclesiastes 12:1:
Remember also your Creator in the days of your youth,
before the evil days come and the years draw near when you
will say, "I have no delight in them";

S olomon exhorts us in this passage to begin serving our Creator early in life before the ravages of time take their toll on our ability to do so. When Solomon refers here to the "evil days", he is referring not to sin but to the years at the end of our lives. It will be difficult to find delight in God if we wait until our final days.

This passage is a stark reminder of the importance of teaching our children and grandchildren at a very young age about the God that created them.

> *This passage is a stark reminder of the importance of teaching our children and grandchildren at a very young age about the God who created them.*

Moses admonished the Israelites to do just that in Deuteronomy 6:5-7:

You shall love the LORD your God with all your heart and with all your soul and with all your might. These words, which I am commanding you today, shall be on your heart. You shall teach them diligently to your sons and shall talk of them when you sit in your house and when you walk by the way and when you lie down and when you rise up.

This, obviously, is sage advice for us as well, particularly in this culture that bombards our children on a daily basis with evolutionary propaganda and anti-God rhetoric designed to pry them away from their Creator and Savior.

The wonders of God's creation and the excitement of discovery by our children will insulate them from the inevitable battles that they will face from the culture if we prepare them properly. Preparing them properly demands our time and attention in order to understand scripture as well as to teach it to our children and grandchildren.

Train up a child in the way he should go, even when he is old he will not depart from it. (Proverbs 22:6)

Lord God, please preserve our children and shelter them from worldly thinking so that their love for You will endure. Amen.

Isaiah 65:17:
"For behold, I create new heavens and a new earth; And the former things will not be remembered or come to mind."

The world in which we live has been cursed (Genesis 3:14-19). As such, today's societies pay little heed to God's word or the things that he commanded of us. The prophet Isaiah, who authored today's passage had condemned Israel for the way they had turned away from morality:

Woe to those who call evil good, and good evil; Who substitute darkness for light and light for darkness; Who substitute bitter for sweet and sweet for bitter! (Isaiah 5:20)

That admonishment is ever so appropriate today. In Paul's letter to the Romans, he tells us this in Chapter 8:22:

"For we know that the whole creation groans and suffers the pains of childbirth together until now."

Paul uses the imagery of a woman in labor to make an important point. As we get closer to the end, the pains will come more frequently and with more intensity. It is difficult to imagine that things will get worse than they are today, but scripture says they will.

> *Paul uses the imagery of a woman in labor to make an important point. As we get closer to the end, the pains will come more frequently and with more intensity.*

Today's verse from Isaiah offers a wonderful ray of hope for followers of Jesus Christ, for a new heaven and earth await those of us who call on the name of the Messiah... and it is glorious:

The curse will be a thing of the past (Revelation 22:3) and God will dwell among us (Revelation 21:3).

Death, mourning, crying and pain will no longer exist (Revelation 21:4).

As believers, we can be secure in the knowledge that we will live for eternity in the presence of the King.

Thank You, Lord that You are a promise-keeping God and that You have ordained our future in Paradise. Amen.

Romans 8:19-21:
For the anxious longing of the creation waits eagerly for the revealing of the sons of God. For the creation was subjected to futility, not willingly, but because of Him who subjected it, in hope that the creation itself also will be set free from its slavery to corruption into the freedom of the glory of the children of God.

*P*aul writes this section of Romans with great anticipation as he is looking forward to the resurrection of the dead and the new heaven and the new earth.

He tells us that the physical universe also awaits this day with anticipation. God himself had subjected the creation to corruption as a result of Adam's sin and all of it was affected. Paul's great message in this passage is that on the day that the *"sons of God are revealed"* they are not alone in being liberated, all of creation will be set free from subjugation to the curse.

> *When that triumphant day occurs, Christ will share His glory with us and all of our earthly trials and tribulations will be a thing of the past.*

What a marvelous day that will be. Paul describes it in 1 Corinthians 15:51-52:

Behold, I tell you a mystery; we will not all sleep, but we will all be changed, in a moment, in the twinkling of an eye, at the last trumpet; for the trumpet will sound, and the dead will be raised imperishable, and we will be changed.

This is Revelation 21:4:

He will wipe away every tear from their eyes; and there will no longer be any death; there will no longer be any mourning, or crying, or pain; the first things have passed away."

When that triumphant day occurs, Christ will share His glory with us in the new heaven and new earth and all of our earthly trials and tribulations will be a thing of the past.

This is Revelation 22:3:

There will no longer be any curse; and the throne of God and of the Lamb will be in it, and His bond-servants will serve Him;

Yes, Lord. We will serve you.

Lord God, we fervently look forward to this glorious day that will be the advent of our eternity with You! Amen.

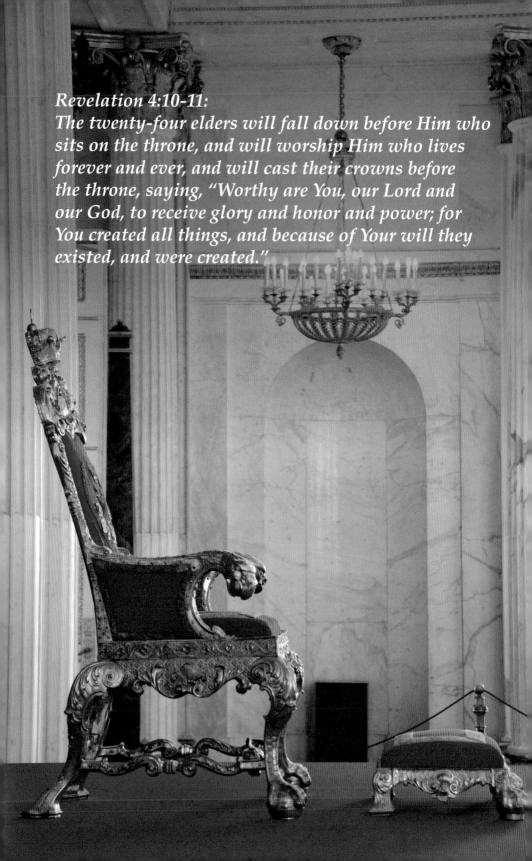

Revelation 4:10-11:
The twenty-four elders will fall down before Him who sits on the throne, and will worship Him who lives forever and ever, and will cast their crowns before the throne, saying, "Worthy are You, our Lord and our God, to receive glory and honor and power; for You created all things, and because of Your will they existed, and were created."

ho exactly are the twenty-four elders referenced in this passage?

Scripture doesn't give us a clear answer and that leaves room for speculation by theologians. One thing we know for sure, they have thrones of their own, they are clothed in white garments and they are each wearing a golden crown (Revelation 4:4), so they are reigning with Christ... and they cast their crowns before the throne of God in acknowledgment that He is responsible for the rewards that they had received. Most fittingly, they then worship.

The list of things for which they could give God praise is endless, yet they choose to praise Him for creation. These elders know that the reason for their very existence is the will of God and their presence there in the throne room is at His discretion.

> These elders know that the reason for their very existence is the will of God and their presence there in the throne room is at His discretion.

1 Corinthians 8:6 says:

"yet for us there is but one God, the Father, from whom are all things and we exist for Him; and one Lord, Jesus Christ, by whom are all things, and we exist through Him."

All of scripture is clear that our existence is from God, through Jesus Christ. It is also clear that our redemption is also from God through Jesus Christ.

Jesus is the Creator, the Messiah and the reigning King.

These twenty-four elders rejoice at their presence in the throne room and they are overcome with the emotion of eternity in the presence of the King.

As redeemed Christians we will also spend eternity in His presence. We will be overcome as well.

Thank you, Lord God that all You created was for our benefit... and thank You that Your love for us is such that You created a path to redemption through the sacrifice of Your Son, Jesus. Truly glory and honor and power are Yours. Amen.

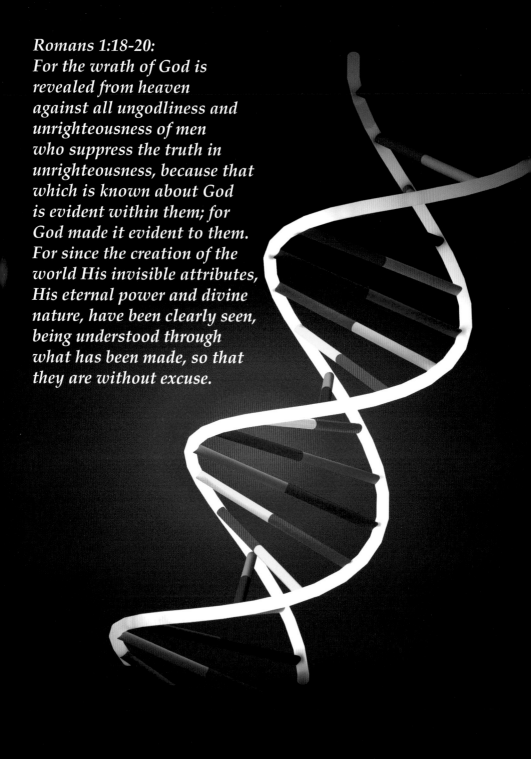

Romans 1:18-20:
For the wrath of God is revealed from heaven against all ungodliness and unrighteousness of men who suppress the truth in unrighteousness, because that which is known about God is evident within them; for God made it evident to them. For since the creation of the world His invisible attributes, His eternal power and divine nature, have been clearly seen, being understood through what has been made, so that they are without excuse.

n the summer of 2009, the Pew Research Center conducted a survey of members of the American Association for the Advancement of Science[19]. Astoundingly, the survey showed this:

- 33% of their members believe in God
- 18% of their members believe in a "universal spirit" or a "higher power"
- 41% did not believe in the existence of God
- 7% were agnostic or refused to answer

Considering the miraculous complexity of every living thing, the countless elements necessary to initiate and sustain life and the harmonious relationships necessary both in nature and in the cosmos that makes it all work, it boggles the mind to realize that only 33% of those who systematically observe and experiment in the various scientific disciplines believe in God.

Think about this: Hemoglobin is a protein that carries oxygen through our bloodstream to our tissues.

Proteins are made up of amino acids, which are made up of molecules which are made up of atoms, the basic unit of matter.

A good way to remember that is this: An atom is a letter, a molecule is a word, an amino acid is a sentence and a protein is a paragraph.

There are 287 amino acids used to build hemoglobin in two separate chains, each chain also having a duplicate. In essence, hemoglobin is a paragraph with 287 sentences (and just like a sentence, structure must be correct). That is quite a paragraph... more like a research paper! It is estimated that there are over 100,000 different proteins (paragraphs) in the human body, all with a different and important function.

Those who do not believe in a Creator are forced to believe that hemoglobin and the thousands of other proteins necessary for life came together randomly with no design or purpose. This is absurd.

Our passage says quite plainly that God has made it evident within them, that they should understand through what has been made and they are without excuse, as are we.

Lord, thank You that You have opened our eyes to the truth and that You have revealed Your glorious creation to us. We are overwhelmed. Amen.

---

[19] https://www.pewforum.org/2009/11/05/scientists-and-belief/

Romans 8:37-39:
But in all these things we overwhelmingly conquer through Him who loved us. For I am convinced that neither death, nor life, nor angels, nor principalities, nor things present, nor things to come, nor powers, nor height, nor depth, nor any other created thing, will be able to separate us from the love of God, which is in Christ Jesus our Lord.

omans Chapter 8 is a wonderful discourse on the sufficiency of Christ and the power of the Holy Spirit in the lives of those who are in Christ.

It starts with Paul encouraging the Roman Christians (and us as well) that there is no condemnation for those who are in Christ and it ends with today's passage in which he tells them that they cannot be separated from the love of Christ.

He unequivocally proclaims their victory, even to the point of listing everything they have overcome, and just in case he missed something, Paul uses the catch-all phrase *"nor any other created thing"*.

Paul uses very powerful rhetoric in this passage. The Greek word for conquer is *hypernikáō*. It literally means "beyond conquer" and the connotation is that Christians have complete and overwhelming victory through Jesus Christ.

> *There is nothing in all of God's creation that can keep a believer from eternity in heaven. Unconditionally and absolutely nothing.*

When Paul says that nothing will be able to separate us from the love of God, the word "separate" is in the Greek aorist tense, meaning that this is a "done-deal".

In John 16:33 Jesus tells his disciples: *"These things I have spoken to you, so that in Me you may have peace. In the world you have tribulation, but take courage; I have overcome the world."*

In John 6:37 Jesus puts an exclamation point on it: *"All that the Father gives Me will come to Me, and the one who comes to Me I will certainly not cast out."*

There is nothing in all of God's creation that can keep a believer from eternity in heaven. Unconditionally and absolutely nothing.

Lord God, it is tremendous encouragement that we are incontrovertibly and eternally Yours and that our position in the heavenly realm is safe and secure in Christ. Amen.

The conclusion, when everything has been heard, is: fear God and keep His commandments, because this applies to every person. For God will bring every act to judgment, everything which is hidden, whether it is good or evil.

Ecclesiastes 12:13-14

Front cover: Photo by Anja from Pixabay

Additional Photo Credits (In Alphabetical Order by Bible Verse):

1 Corinthians 15:45: Photo by VinnyPrime from FreeImages
Acts 17:26: Photo by Nicholas Green from Unsplash
Colossians 1:16: Image by Erich Westendarp from Pixabay
Colossians 2:8: Image from Pixabay
Ecclesiastes 12:1: Photo by Allie Schaefer
Ephesians 2:10: Image by Jackson David from Pixabay
Exodus 20:11: Photo by Hannah Kelsey
Genesis 1:1: Photo by Falk Schaaf from FreeImages
Genesis 1:2: Photo by peejay from FreeImages
Genesis 1:3-5: Photo by Kristin Smith from FreeImages
Genesis 1:9: Photo by Rowey G from FreeImages
Genesis 1:11-12: Image by Rudy and Peter Skitterians from Pixabay
Genesis 1:14: Image by Jpogi at English Wikipedia via Wikimedia
          Commons
Genesis 1:16-18: Photo by David Cowan from FreeImages
Genesis 1:20: Photo by Ozan Uzel from FreeImages
Genesis 1:24: Photo by Justus Kindermann from FreeImages
Genesis 1:26-27: Image by Reimund Bertrams from Pixabay
Genesis 1:28-29: Photo by New York Public Library from Unsplash
Genesis 2:2: Photo by Ferenc Wilmek from Pixabay
Genesis 2:3: Image from Pixabay
Genesis 2:7: Photo by Caroline Hoos from FreeImages
Genesis 2:16-17: Photo by Andy Barton from FreeImages
Genesis 3:15: Photo by Paul Fris from FreeImages
Hebrews 11:3: Image from Wikimedia Commons
Isaiah 45:18: Photo by zuberio from FreeImages
Isaiah 65:17: Image by Carien van Hest from FreeImages
Isaiah 66:1-2: Image by Jesper Noer from FreeImages
Jeremiah 10:12: Photo by Fred Fokkelman from FreeImages
Jeremiah 33:25: Photo by Bryan Wintersteen from FreeImages
Job 12:7-10: Image from Pixabay
Job 38:4-6: Photo by Asif Akbar from FreeImages
John 1:1-3: Photo by dimnitri_c from FreeImages
Matthew 19:4-5: Photo by Nat Arnett from FreeImages
Psalm 8:3-5: Photo by Charlie Balch from FreeImages
Psalm 8:6-8: Photo by William Maury Morris II, via Wikimedia Commons
Psalm 14:1: Image By Bubba73 (Jud McCranie) via Wikimedia Commons
Psalm 19:1-2: Image from NASA